PROJECT MANAGEMENT MASTERY

A COMPREHENSIVE GUIDE TO SUCCESSFULLY
IMPLEMENTING THE CORE PRINCIPLES OF PROJECT
PLANNING AND SCOPE MANAGEMENT FROM
CONCEPT TO COMPLETION

JACK HAYDEN

D1438273

CONTENTS

INTRODUCTION

"Operations keeps the lights on, strategy provides a light at the end of the tunnel, but project management is the train engine that moves the organization forward." — Joy Gumz

---

Project management is a vast world unto itself. Very few professions involve so many intricate management terms, tools, and skills. For starters, there's much to understand, such as planning, budgeting, scheduling, and leadership. For those new to this world, know it is entirely okay to feel overwhelmed. That's good, as this demonstrates the job is taken seriously.

Project managers are great at taking up challenges. But sometimes, they could use some extra encouragement, someone that relates to the struggles of the job. Often, the project manager flies solo in rallying their teams while also taking care of stakeholder concerns. There is oftimes a point in every project when the most helpful thing is a sprinkling of perspective. So, it's good to acknowledge that others understand how challenging this job can be. To achieve success, it is vital to maintain a broad perspective and keep a sharp focus on the bigger picture, and remain open minded to finding motivation from many places.

Management is not a precise science. It is also not an art or a craft, yet, it features core aspects from all three disciplines. It is a Venn diagram where the circles for the three meet and convene as one whole. A project manager needs to be methodical. They must have a mind for budgeting and scheduling in tandem with planning. This plan cannot happen in an abstract realm and requires a motivated project manager to take charge and guide the team to project completion.

In the dynamic realm of project management, external factors can have a significant impact, and the human element of team execution is always a key consideration. As an art, project management demands flexibility, creativity, and astute problem-solving abilities to navigate the complexities and hurdles that arise along the way.

While our world offers many fantastic opportunities, it can also be overwhelming and intimidating for some individuals, particularly when faced with various challenges and demands. Before we let that happen, allow me to share a brief story. Sarah, a young woman, landed her dream job as a marketing manager. She was thrilled because she got to work in a creative environment with a team of talented people. As soon as she began working, she realized project management was more challenging than she'd figured.

A month in, her boss approached her about a big project. The company was planning to launch a brand-new product. Sarah was put in charge of the marketing campaign. She was excited and dove in headfirst, but soon, she felt stressed and overwhelmed. Soon everything had begun spiraling out of control, and she couldn't figure out how to put the team back on track.

Stuck and frustrated at how things were going, Sarah confided in Alex, a friend and successful project manager. Alex listened to her issues and gave her valuable advice that changed the course of her project management journey for good.

"Sarah," he said, "the key to successfully managing any project is all about breaking your project into manageable pieces. It's like eating pizza. It's best enjoyed slice by slice, not all in one go."

At first, Sarah was a little confused. But, the more she thought about it, the more sensible it seemed. She realized that she'd been trying to tackle the entire project all at once instead of breaking it down into smaller, more structured tasks that would feed into one organized whole.

With Alex's help and mentorship, Sarah finally created a project plan that was detailed and achievable. It included all the necessary steps and deadlines, and she assigned specific tasks to different members of her team. Together, the team worked far more efficiently and effectively as they reached the project's end goals.

In essence, that is the power of project management. It may sound daunting, but when it is broken down and taken one step at a time, you'll find it easier to tackle even the most complex of tasks. In this book, I will be sharing with you all the tips and tools you need to become a successful project manager, regardless of your level of experience.

You will learn all about the basics of project management and how to do it from start to finish. The book will equip readers with all the knowledge and tools needed to implement core project management methodologies on different projects. Whether a beginner looking to learn the basics or a seasoned pro looking to fine-tune their skills, this book has it all.

I am an established Contracting and Project Manager with years of experience in large-dollar government systems. I particularly love the complexity and challenging nature of scaling large projects to the point of completion. I've been studying the topic for over two decades, and I'm committed to helping you reach the heights where you can drive your projects regardless of time and cost constraints.

It may seem complicated, but all it takes is perspective and patience. This book will discuss concepts that you can implement quickly and efficiently. It will also talk about how a project manager can manage and motivate team members so that, as a holistic unit, they deliver a successful project without delays or cost overruns.

Our key focus will be successful project delivery, explaining the knowledge and framework of project management from a practitioner's point of view and elucidating a simplified way to learn and execute different project management concepts. Let us begin and dive into the exciting world of project management!

LEARN

THINK

DISCOVER

INVENT

IMAGINE

KNOW

CONSTRUCT

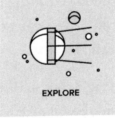

EXPLORE

BUILD

1

PROJECT MANAGEMENT OVERVIEW

P roject managers are akin to orchestra conductors. They work to keep everything moving in smooth sync. They ensure that all different and seemingly uncoordinated parts of an organization come together to build something cohesive, appealing, and top-notch during delivery. In the cut-throat world of business, project managers play a crucial role in ensuring the deliverables are completed on time, within budget, and in a way that meets the objectives of all stakeholders involved.

Project managers bring order to chaos. Projects can be incredibly complex things, and they involve multiple moving parts, teams, and demanding stakeholders. The purpose of having a project manager is to ensure there is someone to coordinate and organize the various moving pieces. Project managers are here to ensure that team members are on the same page. The result is that projects move forward cohesively within time, cost, and the organization's goals.

Another reason project managers are essential is that they provide a singular point of contact. The project manager is the liaison who ensures that everyone communicates effectively. Project managers are crucial for risk management. They are responsible for identifying potential risks and developing strategies to mitigate them. This involves contingency planning, building alternative approaches, or arranging for additional time and resources to take care of potential issues.

As the project manager, an individual will play a vital role in their company's success. It is essential to begin with good foundational knowledge. Just like learning something by understanding its skeletal framework first, in project management, it helps to start by knowing what the discipline stands for.

THE VALUE OF PROJECT MANAGEMENT

Project management is an appealing field for several reasons. To begin with, it's a highly competitive industry. There will always be a demand for competent project managers in a dynamic business environment. Those who choose to work in the field of project management will have more employment options and opportunities to progress in their careers (*Project Management Demand: Career Opportunities,* 2023).

Project management also offers a wide range of potential employment settings. Project managers are very versatile professionals who can work in a number of different fields and take on projects of varying sizes and levels of complexity. In other words, the sector always has room for new developments and discoveries.

Project management is an ever-changing, rewarding environment and offers the opportunity for high earning potential. A lucrative salary is another perk of working in project management. Experienced project managers can command high wages in many fields due to their high demand and competitive skill sets (How Much Do Project Managers Make? 2022).

Project management is essential in a wide range of industries, particularly construction, marketing, and software development to name a few.

A project manager must have strong organizational, leadership, and communication skills to manage teams and work efficiently. They must also understand project management tools and methodologies like the

Waterfall or Agile methods to plan and execute different projects effectively. In essence, project management is the sum of all the processes involving the project's planning, implementation, and completion. Which includes goal-setting, creating a defined timeline with room for modifications, allocating resources, and coordinating the efforts of a team to achieve specific project objectives.

WHAT IS A PROJECT IN RELATION TO PROJECT MANAGEMENT?

As a discipline, project management is centered around planning, organizing, and managing resources to achieve defined goals and objectives. These goals and objectives come together to form a project, and these often operate within a specific timeframe and budget plan. The objective will have a defined beginning and ending. It will include limitations, such as cost, scope, time, and quality.

A project typically encompasses five phases, and these are initiation, planning, execution, monitoring/control, and closure.

Initiation

In the initiation phase, the project manager works with different stakeholders to define the nuances of the project, including objectives, scope, and criteria for success. They also identify the key resources needed to achieve a successful project.

Planning

The planning phase involves the peak period of the operation, where effort is made to develop a detailed project plan that will outline the project's requirements. This phase also helps managers evaluate and develop a risk mitigation plan.

Execution

This is the time for implementing the project plan, managing the team, and ensuring all deliverables get completed to the specified project requirements.

Monitoring and Control

Next is the monitoring/control phase. This is the time for the project manager to monitor the project's progress. They measure performance and take corrective action where necessary.

Closure

The project manager completes the final deliverables, obtains acceptance from relevant stakeholders, and formally closes the project. In this final stage, a post-project review is conducted.

Successful project management calls for well-defined goals, thorough preparation, expert leadership, strict oversight, and active participation from all parties involved. When businesses take a methodical approach to managing their projects, they are more likely to provide results that gratify their stakeholders and achieve their goals (Hardy-Vallee, 2012).

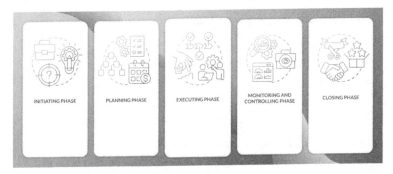

Image: Project Phases

When planning a project, it is essential to consider several constraints that must be acknowledged. The term *triple constraint* describes these boundaries, which consist of time, cost, and amount of work involved. Quality, resources, and risk are just a few of the critical constraints that the project manager must consider. All of the project's limitations are interconnected and can be affected by changes to any of them.

Time

Time is a crucial consideration, as it establishes the duration and deadlines of the project. Time management skills are essential to the completion of any project. In order to ensure that the project is completed on time, it is the project manager's responsibility to create a feasible and practical timetable. If the project manager wants to get things done on time, they need to do the following:

- Define the significant checkpoints and deadlines throughout the project's lifespan.
- Communicate checkpoints and deadlines to the team. This ensures that everyone has the same goals and timeframes to work toward.
- Create a project schedule that specifies the start and end dates of the project, the duration of each task, and the time it may take to obtain necessary resources. The project manager should also add buffers to address problems that may arise along the way.
- Supervise the project's timetable throughout and adjust as needed to avoid delays. The project timeframe may need to be adjusted, resources may need to be reallocated, or new tactics may need to be implemented.

- Use time management tools such as Gantt charts and critical path analysis to visualize the project schedule better, pinpoint the most critical tasks, and keep things on track.

Successful project completion relies heavily on careful time management. The project manager's ability to keep things on track is crucial to completing the project on schedule. Time can make or break the success of any project.

Cost

Another constraint of a project is its cost. Project costs can include the following:

- Total project cost
- Project contract costs
- Equipment
- Facility maintenance
- Material cost

Project Budget

A project budget is a procedural plan detailing the project's expenditures, the account(s) specified for funding, and the billing schedule. It also sets a monetary limitation on what is available to spend.

The project budget is a prospective procedure made in advance of the initiation of the project. It serves as a guideline for monitoring the entire project cost, thus diminishing the risk of exhausting resources, as is common with many projects. A Project Management Institute Pulse Of The Profession report in 2021 stated that 62% of projects in their enterprise met budget targets in the span of a year (PMIl, 2021).

Budgeting allows the project manager to reign in the stakeholders to release much-needed funds. Stakeholders appreciate a detailed expenditure plan to provide project transparency.

Scope

Project scope signifies the attributes, technicalities, and service. The project scope, time, and cost are interdependent elements of a project, and changes in any one can affect the other two.

Project scope sets boundaries and defines precise goals, deadlines, and deliverables. Defining and establishing the project scope ensures timely and seamless fulfillment of the project's goals and objectives.

Unfortunately, *scope creep* can derail even the most stable of projects. Within certain limits, creep can be innocuous. However, significant scope creep can damage a project's success by affecting its objectives. The project manager may devote more time on task mitigation rather than meeting project deadlines.

Scope creep can and will arise at any point during the project's lifecycle. For example, adding product features or functions surpassing the original statement of work can delay and derail a project, even if scope milestones are set. To avoid creep, one must be aware and create a robust project plan and get it approved by the stakeholders before kick-starting it (Martins, 2023).

Undoubtedly, the iron triad of scope, time, and cost is difficult to navigate while maintaining project quality.

Besides the ironclad triad of time, cost, and scope, some other project constraints are risks, resources, and quality.

Risks

Risks, like scope creep, affect a project adversely. Every good project plan includes a proactive risk management strategy to avoid delays and extra costs. During the planning phase, one may conduct stakeholder interviews to gain insights into the potential internal and external risks associated with the current project.

Risk analysis in project management involves identifying, assessing, and managing potential risks to mitigate their impact. Effective risk management strategies can help project managers and their teams anticipate, prepare for, and respond to potential risks that could negatively impact the project's timeline, budget, or quality. By proactively addressing risks, project managers can improve the likelihood of project success and minimize potential consequences. Some risks that a project may encounter are:

- Stretched resources

- Operational mishaps
- Poor performance
- Absence of clarity
- Scope creep
- High costs
- Time shortages

Resources

Resources are assets to ensure proper project management. They include project team members, a sound budget, specialized equipment, and other assets. Resources have cost implications. A deficiency in proper resource allocation can pose a significant threat to project success, leading to compromised quality, delays, and cost overruns.

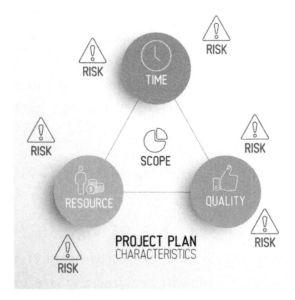

Project Quality

Projects have predetermined expectations, and their quality determines how the project outcomes or deliverables will satisfy them. However, poor quality can occur without any relation to other constraints because:

- Lack of information exchange
- Poor design or development
- A large number of project modifications
- Lack of resources
- Poor leadership

Project quality must be managed as a distinct entity with the triple constraints: time, scope, and cost to obtain high performance. Managing these constraints can lead to poor customer experience due to substandard project quality (6 Project Constraints, 2022).

WHAT DOES PROJECT MANAGEMENT MEAN TODAY?

In the post-pandemic business world, the role of project managers is evolving. A new breed of business ventures called gymnastic enterprises have emerged, which are flexible and can make use of suitable opportunities while maintaining their framework, protocol, and running operations. They choose the best working strategies and employ standardized risk management practices. They also embrace and promote higher organizational agility than traditional organizations. This ensures project success by allowing managers to develop new thinking strategies based on the organization's culture.

Robotic Process Automation (RPA) and predictive analytics technologies mean that conventional project management does not require an extensive human touch, particularly with repetitive features that can be automated.

Even as RPA is gaining traction, the traditional importance of the project manager can never be understated. Many businesses still rely on project managers to carry out routine jobs. Communication, stakeholder negotiation, conflict management, and proactive decision-making will remain indispensable project manager skills. Indeed, job requirements for prospective managers still enlist these aptitudes as desirable skills.

Training for project managers addresses matters like developing a plan, managing dependencies, handling risks, knowing which templates to use, and methods to proceed through the phase gate.

A phase gate (also known as a stage gate or a milestone gate) is a formal review point in a project where key stakeholders assess the project's progress and determine whether it is ready for the next stage. Each gate typically has a set of criteria that must be met before the project can proceed to the next phase.

This approach can minimize risks, identify issues early, and ensure that resources are allocated effectively. It can also help project managers identify and address problems before they become more significant, which can help keep projects on track and budget.

By using phase gates, project managers can ensure that their projects are properly planned, monitored, and controlled throughout their lifecycle. This approach can improve project outcomes, increase stakeholder satisfaction, and enhance the overall project management process. As such, phase gate methodology is often taught as a core component of project management training programs.

In the future, artificial intelligence, like Extreme Programming or XP, can take over the mundane activities of project managers, leaving them to deal with strategic advising, innovating, and communication tasks. Research organizations like Gartner and Forrester predict that in the coming 10 -15 years, project managers' roles will completely evolve to embrace multiple softer skills encompassing a profound understanding of the business and a project's strategic value.

Many businesses spend a vast amount of money on developing soft skills. Soft skills will ensure better connectivity, trusting relationships, and accountability. Communication, teamwork, emotional intelligence, and leadership qualities focusing on team spirit and efficient problem-solving skills are crucial to project completion and are called power skills (Runyon, 2022). Software or A.I. can do the mechanical aspect of managerial tasks, enabling the project manager to address the power skills. For the organization, it would mean efficient use of resources.

Already advanced software can do most of the routine. However, project managers help businesses decide priorities, understand requirements, and maintain clarity. It involves analytical capabilities, emphasizing executive skills, and being an executor of project plans. The future role of project managers will evolve more in that direction.

Businesses will increasingly engage project managers as course deciders. In the near future, project managers will be executive partners in delivering vital organizational functions to enterprises (Bierman, 2019).

PROJECT SEQUENCING

One of the tasks of the project manager is to create project sequencing. This arranges all the tasks in a particular format of sequential order to maintain the flow of the project. In turn, it ensures project efficiency, productivity, and the timely delivery of the final product. Project sequencing benefits can be:

- The implementation of sequencing can improve the quality of work by enhancing the delivery of assignments. A seamless project completion from start to finish will boost team morale, ensure productivity, and generate satisfaction.

- Sequencing can identify and resolve problems. Project managers can follow the timeline and identify things needing attention. Diagnosing and managing problems is easier with project sequencing.

Create a Project Outline

A project outline is a simplified adaptation of the lengthy and exhaustive project plan. The outline details the significant elements of the plan in an easy-to-read and easy-to-follow manner. Outlines can be a project manager's best ally when correctly made.

Consider the project's scope, range, and timeline to know how to start and finish the sequence. The aim is to generate one hundred percent client or customer satisfaction.

Organize the Steps Chronologically

After outlining the different steps, arrange them sequentially according to the timeline. Allocate identification numbers to help the team members understand which tasks must be completed before others. Scheduling the steps according to a timeline helps to finish the tasks methodically. Approaching steps in chronological order can come to one's aid. For instance, if a client asks for another correction before the delivery of the final product, it is easier to locate the position to add the requested procedure.

Set Objectives for Each Step Completion

Establishing rules helps to set quality standards for both preceding and subsequent work. Depending on the project, one may decide upon the relationships between each task. For example, consider working on several different tasks in unison to meet client deadlines. A sequence delineates the orderly connections between different steps of work. For instance, to cook rice, one has to *measure* rice in a vessel, *wash* it, add the *correct* quantity of water, and set it to *boil*. All four activities are to occur in this exact sequence so that one can identify the critical tasks and prioritize them. Using the sequence to quality check before transitioning to the next step can be helpful in many situations.

Create a Diagram of the Outline

Use the task identification numbers and arrange the tasks sequentially to create a diagram for easy understanding. Choose shapes and patterns easily identifiable by team members to know each task component's beginning and end. For example, a circle between two shapes may indicate a finish-to-start relationship; if an arrow passes through the circle, it may mean that the members can begin with the following tasks. However, they need to finish the preceding tasks first. Set deadlines for each task and convey them to the team to check project constraints. The sequence diagram illustrates the following types of tasks:

- **Finish-to-start** means the following action can only start if the previous one is completed.
- **Finish-to-finish** means team members can complete the following task when the first one is complete. For example, webpage construction is only finished when the website coding is finalized.
- **Start-to-start:** means a successor can start their work after the predecessor has started. For instance, the designers can start designing the website once its coding has also begun.
- **Start-to-finish:** means the following task cannot finish until the primary task begins.

Distribute the Diagram to Team Members

To ensure project success, the team must adhere to the project objectives. After task distribution, motivate team members to understand and follow the sequence components depicted in the diagram for which they are responsible. For instance, when the project manager assigns steps one and two, it indicates that the team needs to work on the initial half of the project.

Sharing the list of assigned work is helpful for the team members. It will enable members to locate who is responsible for the preceding and the successive task components. The diagram allows them to communicate with the right individual while completing their tasks, thus creating an efficient team.

Some tips for project sequencing are as follows:

- Make an overall but thorough plan even if it is impossible to forecast all the tasks the project may need. Use resources to make measurable and precise targets and create a streamlined and flexible sequence.
- Emphasize the work schedule of the team members by placing effective timelines that bring out the best in everyone. The goals must be practical and encouraging to the team members.
- Discuss the project sequence with everyone on the team to ensure they understand it fully. Ultimately, individual tasks add up to the whole, and deficiency in one can affect the entire project.

- Use project management software for better productivity. The apps can help design and share project sequences with team members (What Is Project Sequencing, 2021).

PROJECT MANAGEMENT FUNDAMENTALS: AN OVERVIEW

Typically, a project consists of the following phases:

- Initiation phase
- Preparation or planning phase
- Execution phase
- Monitoring and control phase
- Closing phase

A project concept can stem from a problem that requires resolution or an opportunity that necessitates further exploration. A project may arise for many reasons, but all projects set out to resolve, create, and complete something. The initiation phase of the project marks the beginning of this process.

Initiation Phase

First, an expert team assesses the project's viability through studies on feasibility, cost-benefit analysis, project scope, deliverables, and stakeholders. A project charter, created by the project sponsor, is the most important document in this phase. Once approved, the project plan is prepared in the planning process, saving time, money and ensuring quality.

The charter authorizes the project and highlights three key features: scope, objectives, and responsibilities. It can contain references to the following aspects of the project:

- Business vision and mission
- Project goals and value to the business
- List of stakeholders
- Project deliverables
- Project scope and budget
- Risks

Let us quickly review how a project charter differs from a project plan. A project plan represents a detailed document outlining the tasks, timelines, and resources required to complete a project. It includes project scope, budget, risks, and quality assurance information and is created after the project charter.

On the other hand, a project charter is a high-level document that outlines the project's goals, objectives, stakeholders, and high-level requirements. It is usually created at the beginning of a project and serves as a guide for the project team to ensure they align with the overall project vision.

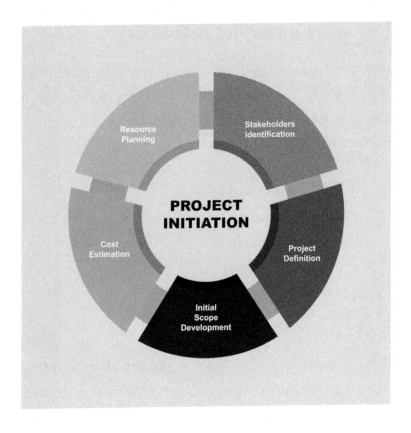

In summary, a project plan provides a detailed roadmap for executing a project. In contrast, a project charter sets the foundation for the project by defining its purpose and scope.

Preparation or Planning Phase

In this phase, the project is established, and the project manager coordinates official aspects. Staff selection, project planning, and budget preparation take place. The project manager analyzes requirements, plans effective sequencing, and conducts risk analysis with mitigation planning for execution and monitoring phases.

Effective planning plays a crucial role in determining the results and risks associated with the project. The plan is a reference and guideline to follow through the project phases meticulously and is a must for successful project management. It depicts the targets, objectives, methodologies, and responsibilities of every individual involved with the project. The project manager must understand the project objectives in order to communicate and lead the project team to a successful project completion. The documents developed during the planning phase include the following:

- Statement of Work
- Work breakdown structure (WBS)
- Project Plan
- Project schedule
- Change request form
- Communication plan

- Project quality plan
- Acceptance plan
- Risk analysis and mitigation plan

Execution Phase

The execution phase brings the project to fruition by systematically undertaking tasks from start to finish. The outcomes depend on the project objectives. This is the longest and most complex stage, with many activities running in a compact sequence while maintaining quality and on-time delivery.

The team uses the Work Breakdown Structure (WBS) and project schedule to perform the tasks in the project plan. WBS is a tool to break down tasks into more manageable and doable forms. Frequent team meetings on project progress, assessing project variances, considering change requests, or updating project plans are other features of this project phase.

The project manager must maintain good communication with all the team members and the stakeholders, keeping them informed on the project's progress using status reports and meetings.

Visualization tools play a critical role in project management, enabling project managers and stakeholders to track progress. Specifically, visually represent the timeline, allowing users to identify important milestones and track the movement toward these goals.

Using visualization tools, project managers can quickly identify areas where progress is lagging, and take corrective action to ensure that the project stays on track. Additionally, stakeholders can gain valuable insights into the project's overall performance, allowing them to make informed decisions about resource allocation and project priorities.

One of the crucial benefits of visualization tools is that they allow project managers to communicate project status to stakeholders easily. Rather than relying on lengthy reports or technical documents, project managers can provide stakeholders with a clear, concise visual representation of the project's progress. This helps to ensure that everyone involved in the project understands what needs to be done to achieve success.

Overall, visualization tools are a critical component of modern project management. By providing a clear and intuitive way to track project progress, these tools help to ensure that projects stay on track and deliver value to stakeholders.

Monitoring Phase

The objectives are to ensure the project is on the right track within the confines of its scope. Risks are minimal when a project progresses in the right direction. During the monitoring phase, the project's performance is compared to its planned performance to identify discrepancies, allowing for necessary remediation.

Project Closing Phase

It is the final phase of a project. The closing phase typically lasts for a few weeks or months. However, it is repleted with a flurry of activities. Last-minute revisions and corrections are made, and the finishing touches are applied to ensure client or customer satisfaction. This is the phase when errors can mean disaster. On top of everything, the project deadline is still looming around the bend. Some examples of closing phase activities:

- Guarantee work completion.
- Project review/lessons learned
- Formally recognizing project completion by all stakeholders.

The project manager and their team members collaborate and review project events and share their individual experiences and perspectives. The whole lifecycle of the project is summed up to draw inferences, learn lessons, recognize areas of improvement, determine mutual strengths, and identify weaknesses. All these are documented together with project information for future reference (Simplilearn, 2023).

BROADER PROJECT ILLUSTRATION

Team Structure

A project team is a multifunctional group working to achieve a common target. Besides the project manager who leads the team, the team comprises team leaders from departments relevant to the project and team members.

The nature of teamwork depends on the organizational structure of the project, which can be of three types, depending on the extent of control given to the project manager and team configuration. The three team structures and their descriptions are as follows:

Project-Based Team Structure

The conventional project-based team structure has the project manager as the authority; all team members report to them. The project manager creates a project plan, the schedule, assigns tasks to team members and supervises the tasks. As this structure is entirely based on the project.

Functional Project Team Structure

Multiple project managers supervise team members' work to achieve specific organizational tasks like marketing or sales. Each team leader has a group of individuals assigned to them. The different categories are arranged according to a predetermined set of criteria called tiers. The team members report to their leaders, who, in turn, must inform the proceedings to the project manager at the top of the chain.

Matrix-Based Project Team Structure

It is a hybrid of project-based and functional project team structures. More prominent corporations use a matrix-based project structure for program functioning and designing project portfolios requiring complex leadership structures like executives, functional managers, program managers, and portfolio managers. The project manager has less control and heads a team that reports to other relevant leaders.

Forming the Project team

The organization and formation of a project team are as vital to the project. The general steps to form a project team involve the following features:

Choosing a Cross-Functional Staff: Cross-functional staff can bring diverse perspectives and skill sets to a project for effective goal achievement. For instance, film projects typically comprise several departments contributing to the production process. All the departments work with the same objective: making a film. The film, in this case, is the deliverable objective. Each department is supervised by a leader managing a team. Hence, the first step to forming the project team would be to decide the department categories and their respective leaders.

The charter or other project planning tools like a responsibility assignment matrix and a Responsible, Accountable, Consulted, and Informed chart, otherwise known as RACI chart, can contain information about the *roles and duties* of the team members assigned by the project manager. This tool provides information on who has the relevant responsibilities and who was consulted or informed about a concerning matter. It mitigates mismanagement and lack of accountability.

Project managers of successful projects establish rules, explain the project keystones, and set clear boundaries from the beginning. Document these rules and objectives and share them among team members for a successful endeavor.

Project targets and aims: The project stakeholders and the team members should know the targets and aims of the project, just as they know their roles in it. Explain project constraints, anticipations, and intentions to ensure as the project manager you establish clear expectations for what the project will achieve, how it will be accomplished, and what potential challenges may arise.

Communication Strategy: A project can only survive well with effective communication. A lack of communication strategy will destroy the cohesiveness of a project. In order to achieve success, a project requires cohesion and collaboration among its various departments, rather than operating as disjointed entities within the organization.

The way to achieve unified functionality is by organizing project meetings, demanding status reports, fixing timings for interdepartmental collaborations, and other methods of interactions (Malsam, 2023).

VALUE OF PROJECT MANAGEMENT

Global businesses are actively seeking competent and experienced professionals who possess a mastery of cutting-edge methodologies and the expertise in niche fields necessary for effectively managing their projects. They seek project managers for their strategic methods, resourcefulness, organizational and motivating capabilities.

Not only do project managers enjoy excellent salaries and engaging, creative work, but their roles also involve skillfully leveraging resources and collaborating with diverse groups to achieve results. However, there is much more to the job than just these benefits. As the industry evolves, project managers are presented with emerging challenges that add to the excitement of their roles and provide invaluable opportunities for personal and professional growth.

Mastering the iron triangle of time, budget, and project scope is a challenging feat, but with dedication and practice, it can be accomplished by anyone. While software skills are undoubtedly critical for success in project management, essential aspects such as team spirit, motivation, visionary leadership, empathetic supervision, and collaboration with project partners cannot be overlooked. As such, it is apparent that the future of project management remains promising and secure as long as professionals recognize the value of developing a broad range of skills beyond just technical proficiency. Project managers *add value* to the project in the following ways:

Tactical Alignment

Tactical project management will see the project all the way from initiation to closing phases, using the finest practices of the Project Management Institute (PMI).

Tactical alignment in project management refers to the process of ensuring that project objectives and deliverables are consistent with the broader goals and strategies of an organization. This requires project managers to align the project's purpose and objectives with the organization's overall vision and mission, as well as with other ongoing projects and initiatives. Effective tactical alignment is essential for ensuring that the project contributes meaningfully to the organization's success and is not simply a standalone effort. By aligning projects with the broader organizational context, project managers can ensure that the project outcomes are relevant, valuable, and impactful.

Leadership

Project managers play a critical role in guiding their teams toward success. They provide valuable leadership by setting a clear direction for the project, motivating team members, and creating a positive work environment that fosters collaboration and innovation.

Effective project managers lead by example, demonstrating the behaviors and values that they expect from their team members. They provide clear guidance and direction, ensuring that team members understand their roles and responsibilities and are equipped with the resources and support needed to accomplish their tasks.

Project managers also act as coaches and mentors, sharing their knowledge and experience with team members to help them develop their skills and grow professionally. They foster an environment of continuous learning and improvement, encouraging team members to seek new challenges and opportunities for growth.

Overall, project managers provide invaluable leadership by guiding and supporting their teams throughout the project lifecycle, helping to ensure that projects are completed successfully and meet the needs of stakeholders.

Clarity of Focus And Objectives

Achieving clarity of focus and objectives is a critical element of effective project management. By defining clear project objectives and ensuring alignment with the organization's overall strategy and goals, project managers can create a shared understanding of what success looks like and enable their teams to work towards a common goal.

To achieve clarity and focus, project managers must first develop a clear project plan that outlines the project scope, timeline, budget, and resource requirements. They should also establish a clear communication strategy to ensure that team members, stakeholders, and sponsors are all aware of project goals and progress.

Achieving clarity and focus of objectives is essential for successful project management. By developing clear project plans, communicating effectively, and prioritizing objectives, project managers can create a shared vision and enable their teams to work towards a common goal, leading to successful project outcomes.

Practical Planning

Effective planning is a crucial aspect of project management, and project managers play a key role in establishing a practical plan that aligns with project objectives and is acceptable to all stakeholders.

Project managers must establish a reasonable timeline and milestones for the project. They work with stakeholders to understand project goals and objectives, assess and adjust resources based on the timeline, identify resources for each task, and develop a plan to allocate resources effectively while considering any constraints or limitations. They must also monitor progress toward milestones and adjust plans to keep the project on track.

By establishing a practical plan that aligns with project objectives and is acceptable to all stakeholders, project managers can help ensure the project is completed on time and within budget. Overall, effective practical planning is critical for successful project management, and project managers must work closely with stakeholders to develop a realistic and achievable plan that is aligned with project objectives.

Quality Control

Quality control in project management is the process of ensuring that project deliverables meet the required quality standards. It involves identifying quality requirements, defining quality criteria, and establishing quality assurance processes to ensure that these criteria are met. Quality control is a continuous process that begins in the planning phase and continues throughout the project's execution and closure. It includes activities such as inspection, testing, and review to identify defects or errors and take corrective action to ensure that the final deliverables meet the expected quality standards. Quality control aims to minimize defects and errors, reduce rework, and ensure that project outcomes meet the customer's expectations.

Risk Management and Supervision

Project managers are well-versed in risk management and proactively assess and address potential risks to ensure success. They are responsible for assigning tasks to the appropriate team members, ensuring that the project is progressing on schedule and within budget.

To maintain the integrity of the project lifecycle, project managers continuously track the project's progress, allowing for timely course corrections if necessary. They are skilled in providing convenient status reports to stakeholders that track project progress and ensure expectations are met.

By effectively managing risks, assigning tasks to the right people, and keeping stakeholders satisfied, project managers build trust with clients and increase the chances of project success. They are crucial in ensuring that projects are completed on time, within budget, and to the desired quality standards.

PROJECT MANAGEMENT

Team Guide

As team guides, project managers often possess subject matter expertise that allows them to provide valuable guidance to team members on niche subjects or tasks. By sharing their knowledge, project managers can help team members identify their strengths and learn from their mistakes, gaining valuable experience.

The final documentation of the "do's and don'ts" is a valuable resource for prospective projects (Aston, n.d.). Preparing this type of documentation serves as a reference guide for best practices and potential pitfalls. With the help of project managers, team members can develop their skills, improve their performance, and contribute to the success of the project.

SUMMARY

Here is a quick overview of what was covered in this chapter.

- Project management is centered around planning, organizing, and managing resources to achieve defined goals and objectives.
- The organization and formation of a project team are as vital to the project as appointing project employees.
- Project managers guide, lead, set examples, motivate, address problems, coach, and share experiences with the team members.
- Project managers assign roles to team members, ensure the timely delivery of tasks and maintain the flow of work.

The next chapter will focus on different foundations of project management, a focus on critical components that make the profession what it is.

2

FOUNDATIONS OF PROJECT MANAGEMENT

This chapter will discuss different aspects of project management strategies for designing a systematized, cohesive, and streamlined roadmap for project execution and management. This section will discuss different topics on project management, highlighting the key concepts and the skills which are essential for the profession.

The chapter has topics on making sharp and precise project objectives, critical project management methodologies and their implementation techniques, different roles of a project lifecycle, and many more issues.

PROJECT VISION

Project vision refers to a clear and concise description of the intended outcome of a project. It outlines the ultimate goal, purpose, and direction of the project and should serve as a guiding principle throughout the project management process. Project vision should help stakeholders, project managers, and team members to align their efforts and make decisions that support the project's overall objectives.

In project management, the project vision is an important element of the project charter. The project charter should establish the project vision, objectives, scope, stakeholders, and overall approach of the project. The project vision serves as a reference point for the project team throughout the project's lifespan, helping them stay on course and maintain their focus on achieving the project objectives. It also provides a framework for evaluating project success, as achieving the project vision is the ultimate measure of success.

PROJECT OBJECTIVES

Project objectives refer to specific, measurable, and time-bound goals that the project team aims to achieve. It provides a clear and achievable target that guides the project's planning, execution, and monitoring processes. The project objective should be aligned with the project vision. Throughout the project lifecycle, the project objective serves as a reference point for the project team to ensure that they remain targeted on delivering the intended results. It also is a helpful tool to evaluate the project's progress, success, and short-comings, as it provides a concrete measure of the project's accomplishments during the project lifecycle. All projects must have a project objective, irrespective of the methodology used. Project objectives, therefore, must be measurable and have key performance indicators (KPIs). Objective and Key Results (OKR) are simple tools that measure the objectives and the key results.

The objectives represent the required outcomes or targets that the team needs to achieve, while the key results are the measurable indicators that show progress towards the desired objectives. Together, objectives and key results provide a clear and actionable plan for achieving success. OKRs are useful tools for setting and tracking goals, aligning team efforts, and ensuring accountability. They allow teams to concentrate on the core requirements and make insight-driven decisions to achieve project success.

Key Performance Indicators (KPIs)

KPIs are metrics that evaluate progress toward the ultimate goals of an organization, and hence each enterprise has its own KPI specific to its goals and objectives. These metrics serve to pinpoint areas for improvement, enabling organizations to make strategic plans based on concrete data. By measuring progress towards established KPIs, companies can identify strengths and weaknesses, set achievable targets, and track their performance over time. KPIs are valuable tools for aligning objectives with outcomes, prioritizing initiatives, and measuring success. Large organizations typically use KPIs to track performance and measure success across various business units. For smaller businesses, KPIs serve a similar purpose but may focus more on progress assessment and resource allocation.

Aims of Project Objectives

Project objectives serve the following purposes:

- Devising project strategies to work toward goals
- Tracking project progress
- Offering guidance to the project team during the project lifecycle
- Gaining stakeholder approvals

Comparison of Goals and Objectives

Both goals and objectives are statements related to the project, but goals are broader in scale, whereas objectives are more precisely defined.

More than one project may be necessary to fulfill the comprehensive and overarching goals. For instance, if the goal of a company is to achieve eco-friendly products, it may require multiple projects involving new processes, training, reorganization, or conversion of the existing systems to achieve the overall mission. Each project would have its own objectives, working toward the ultimate goal.

To produce eco-friendly products, an objective a business might have is to obtain necessary training within the second fiscal quarter, or Q2, which is a great example of using the **S**pecific, **M**easurable, **A**chievable, **R**elevant, and **T**ime-bound (SMART).

Goals and objectives are distinct yet complementary elements of a well-defined plan. While goals represent the long-term outcomes an organization hopes to achieve, objectives are specific, measurable, and foreseeable milestones that help to track progress toward those goals.

Goals are indirectly linked to business cost, time, and product or service standards and must mean something for the business to support or initiate projects. They are measurable but less detailed than business objectives. They help the project manager understand how their projects work toward the ultimate business goals.

Objectives are related to *project* deliverables, which in the previous example, was necessary training of the staff. Objectives have a more clear-cut scope than business or organization's goals. However, statements on the characteristics and operations of a deliverable are *requirements*, not objectives.

To achieve goals and objectives, the project manager plans strategies, and ultimately, the roadmap to success. Conversely, tactics are the specific methods and approaches adopted to execute a job or achieve an objective.

Features	Goals	Objectives
Meaning	Goals address the long-term values of a business or organization.	Objectives describe the specific tasks required to work toward the goal.
Duration	Goals may take longer to accomplish.	Objectives are short or mid-term accomplishments.
Structure	Goals are more generalized and can require multiple projects to achieve.	Objectives are clear-cut and align with the organization's immediate or mid-term achievements.
Measurement criteria	The measurement criteria for goals are more approximate.	Objectives have measurable criteria to evaluate achievements.

Goals and objectives must be clearly defined at the beginning of a project lifecycle to set key performance indicators to track the project's success. Also, goals and objectives act like roadmaps for frequent reference of the project status, without which the project may fail.

How to Make Robust Progress Objectives

To make project objectives credible, review the project goals to get an overall concept of the organization's needs for the project. The objectives should outline specific milestones to achieve those goals. Also, consider the viewpoints of the customers or clients. For example, in a hospital project, it is essential to consider the satisfaction of both patients and visitors by identifying their needs and desires, such as improving waiting areas and providing access to drinking water facilities. Consider asking for their views and feedback as metrics for further improvements. Thus, a project manager identifies the project objectives through data analysis and feedback. Input from customers, clients, and team members can be valuable in defining project objectives.

Another tool that can prove useful in devising a robust project objective is to use SMART. The SMART method stands for Specific, Measurable, Achievable, Relevant, and Time-bound. It is a framework used to set clear and well-defined objectives or goals in a way that increases the likelihood of achieving them.

Specific: Objectives should address the requirements. Consider the five W's: who, what, where, when, and why. To make a comprehensive outline, utilize the five W's with emphasis on the *why* because asking why is crucial to discovering the best possible course of action. The objectives should be clearly defined and specific, remembering to answer questions such as What needs to be achieved? Who is involved? Where will it happen? Why is it important?

Measurable: A scalable objective helps in assessing the progress of the project and understanding when the objective has been achieved. Objectives should be quantifiable, allowing for the measurement of progress and success. This includes identifying relevant metrics to track and measure progress toward the defined objectives. Using KPIs as a tool can be used to measure project objectives by identifying specific metrics that reflect progress toward achieving those objectives.

Achievable: To achieve the project objectives success-fully, it is imperative that the project manager and team members collaborate and design objectives that are realistic and achievable within the available resources. Involving clients/stakeholders and team members in the objective-setting process can help ensure that everyone is aligned with the correct project objectives and committed to working towards them together.

Relevant: When objectives are achievable, they are also realistic. Relevant objectives keep the project aligned with the business goals.

Time-bound: Objectives should have a specific timeline or deadline, creating a sense of urgency to ensure that progress is made toward achieving the objective within a specific timeframe. Projects cannot continue for indefinite periods. After enough time passes, objectives lose their significance. The devised timeframe should be realistic and aligned with the objectives and requirements of the project. It is important to consider factors such as available resources, scope, and complexity of the project when determining a reasonable timeframe. Additionally, the deadline should be flexible enough to allow for unforeseen circumstances or unexpected changes in the project plan. By establishing a reasonable and suitable deadline, project managers can help ensure that the project remains on track and that all stakeholders are satisfied with the progress and outcomes. Objectives must relate precisely to the goals (Goals vs Objective, 2021).

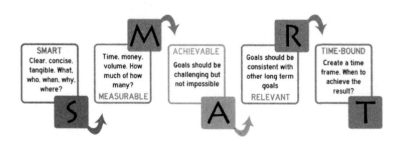

SMART Goals

The 5 Whys technique

Taiichi Ohno, one of the technical founders of the Toyota Motor Corporation, described the strategy of 5 whys in production management. He believed that asking "why" five times solves the issue automatically. Sakichi Toyoda popularized the technique (Usmani, 2022). Let us try an example to see how self-evident the subject is.

Statement: Customer complaints have increased recently.
1st Why?
Statement: They are not receiving their deliverables on time.
2nd Why?
Statement: It is taking longer for production.
3rd Why?
Statement: Frequent malfunctioning machinery.
4th Why?
Statement: Lack of proactive maintenance.
5th Why?
Statement: The contract for maintenance expired and was not renewed.

The following table highlights the utility and the limitations of the 5 Why technique.

Utility	Limitations
It can help to locate more issues while addressing a problem area of the performance.	Having too many people involved in the decision-making process can lead to confusion and complexity, resulting in a lack of clarity and direction.
Motivate active participation and brainstorming by the team members.	Team members must be well-versed in the subject matter and experts in the field.
It is efficient and easy to use.	The main cause may remain unsolved.
It identifies the cause rather than skimming the symptoms.	This approach can be too narrow thinking and miss broader systemic issues.
It prevents knee-jerk reactions that can be counterproductive or pointless for the situation.	In more complex projects, this approach might over-simplify the problem and its causes.
It fosters an environment of continuous improvement.	This approach only works when there is enough data to analyze.

How to Write a Good Project Objective

Recognize Modifiable Behaviors or Factors

Managing internal issues and team member behaviors is critical for the success of any project, as they can have a significant impact on the project's outcomes. One effective approach is to conduct an evaluation of past projects to identify conditions or behaviors that may have contributed to the project's success or failure.

For example, if a previous project was not completed on time due to conflicts between team members, a manager may need to implement conflict resolution strategies or adjust the team's selection for future projects. Alternatively, if a project was completed successfully, identifying what conditions or behaviors led to its success can provide insight into the project management approach for future endeavors.

By analyzing past projects, managers can make informed decisions about how to manage internal issues and team member behaviors in a way that promotes project success. This approach also promotes continuous improvement by learning from past experiences and applying those lessons to future projects.

What is Success?

In order to set SMART objectives, project managers must have a clear understanding of what constitutes success for the project. This involves defining the specific goals and outcomes that the project aims to achieve, as well as identifying the metrics that will be used to measure success.

By understanding the meaning of success for the project, project managers can establish objectives that are specific, measurable, achievable, relevant, and time-bound (SMART). This framework ensures that project objectives are clear, quantifiable, and aligned with the overall goals of the project.

When setting SMART objectives, it is important to consider factors such as available resources, stakeholder expectations, and potential risks and challenges.

Project managers should also ensure that objectives are realistic and attainable within the given timeframe.

Setting SMART objectives can help project managers ensure project focus and success in achieving goals and delivering value to stakeholders. Success can mean different things to different people, so it's important for the team to clearly understand what it means for the organization. Utilizing the SWOT analysis technique can identify project strengths, weaknesses, opportunities, and threats. This helps gain a better understanding of concerns and potential outcomes, defining the key factors contributing to project success.

Time and Place

Time and place are important considerations when writing project objectives because they help to establish a clear and realistic context for the project.

Time refers to the specific timeframe in which the project needs to be completed or specific milestones that need to be achieved. It is important to set realistic deadlines and timelines to ensure that the project stays on track and that all objectives are met within the given time frame. This helps to prevent delays and ensures that the project is completed in a timely and efficient manner.

Place refers to the physical location or environment where the project will take place. This can include factors such as the availability of resources, the local community, and the physical infrastructure necessary to support the project. Understanding the place where the project will take place is important for ensuring that the project is tailored to the specific needs and constraints of the local context, which can help raise the chances of success.

By considering time and place when writing project objectives, you can create a more comprehensive and effective plan that is tailored to the specific needs and challenges of the project.

Simplify the Project Objectives

Project objectives typically provide a plethora of information, but the key is to present them clearly and concisely. Consider breaking them down into shorter, manageable segments. Generate multiple project objectives and choose the most effective ones, using precise statements that focus on practical and scalable targets. Some practices of efficient project objective writing can be:

- Composing the objective before beginning the project

- Determine all the objectives before designing the project charter
- Make short, effective sentences using simple terms (it will be read and appreciated)
- Avoid ambiguity. Mention the things required and needed to fulfill the mission
- Ensure the organization's control of the project objective

The success of a project hinges on clear and specific project goals, strict adherence to project objectives, and timely completion of those objectives. It's crucial to tailor project objectives to the specific project at hand, ensuring they are relevant and achievable within the project's scope. Project success is determined by the specific objectives achieved by project managers and team members.

Business objectives are overarching goals that span a longer period and align with the organization's vision and strategy, often encompassing growth, profitability, market share, and customer satisfaction, with high-level management typically setting these targets. Project managers take these business objectives and seek to incorporate the ultimate mission into each project objective.

In contrast to business objectives, specific project objectives have a narrower focus and are directly tied to the goals and outcomes of a particular project, with unique targets set for delivering a specific product or service, attaining a desired level of quality or efficiency, or meeting a designated deadline or budget constraint.

While business objectives may provide the overarching context for a project, specific project objectives provide a sustainable roadmap for achieving the project's required outcomes. By aligning project objectives with business objectives, organizations can ensure that their projects contribute to achieving their overall strategic goals.

Key Project Management Aspects

Integration Management

Project integration management is essential for coordinating all aspects of a project, including planning, execution, monitoring, and controlling, to achieve its objectives successfully. It involves managing project dependencies, components, and activities, aligning with organizational goals, and ensuring cohesive and efficient work toward desired outcomes.

A crucial step in establishing the project plan involves first developing a project charter. The *project charter* signals the start of the project. It comprises the initial roles, responsibilities, objectives, project goals, and project manager selection. It is a generalized reference document for the project. It is key to note here that project charters do not undergo alterations once initiated. While one may change the contents of a project depending on contingencies, the charter remains fixed. The charter is made by a stakeholder or by the project manager.

The project management plan is built to form a project roadmap, and the sponsors or the stakeholders sanction the project plan. The project management plan is the formal document that defines the approach, processes, and strategies that will be utilized to initiate, plan, execute, monitor, control, and close a project. The project management plan essentially provides the roadmap for the project team to follow and serves as a guide for stakeholders to understand how the project will be executed and controlled. Software like ProjectManager is useful for tracking project plans.

Project integration combines and coordinates various project management processes and activities to achieve objectives. It includes developing a project charter, creating a project management plan, and coordinating project execution, monitoring, and control. The project manager deftly deals with interdependencies in the project management domains, strengthening collaboration across several projects simultaneously.

For a project manager, effective project integration ensures that all project components work together seamlessly, leading to successful project delivery. It also enables the project manager to identify potential problems, develop solutions before they become critical issues, and ensure project outcomes meet stakeholder expectations. In summary, project integration constitutes an essential aspect of project management that helps project managers effectively plan, execute, monitor, and control project activities to achieve project goals. Integration covers the following aspects for effective resource utilization, schedule monitoring, and seamless continuation of operations.

The *project roadmap* is a guide that visually represents the bigger picture of the project, its milestones, tasks, timelines, and deliverables. It explains the different phases of the project. The roadmap includes the scope, risk, and resource management data. Due to its nature, it is an efficient communication mode between all concerned in the project.

In integration management, activities like review meetings, lessons learned reports, change requests, and change control are all important. While some aspects of a project may be difficult to manage, proactive changes can be negotiated and integrated into the overall plan. Project managers must address all changes that affect the project baseline and manage them using the change control methodology, which involves tracking the change and documenting any approved changes.

Project Scope Management

Scope management involves gathering all the specifications for the completed product or service. The project's scope is highlighted in a scope statement, written briefly and precisely, preferably in a bulleted list to emphasize the vital points. The scope statement can change to accommodate alterations during the project lifecycle to control the scope. Scope Management minimizes project risks if implemented properly.

The *work breakdown structure* (WBS) creation is part of scope management.

Scope validation ensures that all the project deliverables and requirements defined in the scope statement have been completed and delivered as intended. It involves reviewing project work products, assessing their completeness and accuracy, and comparing them against the project scope to confirm that they meet the project's needs.

Scope validation is a necessary project management process that ensures that the project outcomes align with stakeholder expectations and that the project has been successfully completed. It enables project managers to identify gaps or deficiencies in the project work and to take corrective actions to address them, ensuring that the project is delivered successfully and meets the desired objectives.

The controlling process enables the project manager to keep the project moving in the right direction and handle changes to the supply chain, client demand, and related variables that determine the company's overall mission. By using scope verification techniques, the project manager can monitor the overall health of the project deliverables. Some commonly used techniques that are useful to the project manager are inspection and review of the project deliverables, testing of project deliverables prior to signing off at acceptance, gaining peer reviews, and stakeholder walk-throughs prior to project close.

Other strategies of scope management include:

- Work breakdown structures
- Mind maps
- Statements of work
- Requirements analysis

- Scope management plans
- Scope change controls

Time Management

The project is broken down into time-bound tasks, with start dates, deadlines, and budgets for each task. As things constantly evolve in the project lifecycle, timelines may need to be revised using *plan schedule management*, which creates a schedule and determines the individual(s) responsible for a particular assignment. Activities thus get defined in a similar way as a WBS.

A *task list* touches on all aspects of the project. The tasks are arranged sequentially for bigger projects, with an awareness of the dependencies between them. The dependencies are categorized as finish-to-start (FS), finish-to-finish (FF), start-to-start (SS), or start-to-finish (SF).

Task durations are determined to create a schedule, which requires finding out the critical path and float of each task. A Gantt chart is used to position the tasks on a timeline, and each task's *resource requirement* is appraised and procured.

The *schedule* requires a management plan. *Earned value management* ensures the current project is progressing as intended.

Critical Path and Float

The critical path refers to the longest duration required to complete a project, spanning from its initiation to its culmination. It indicates the minimum time that must be allocated for the project's successful completion.

Float, or slack, is how much a project can be delayed before it starts to impact the specified project deadlines.

Project Cost Management

To effectively manage project costs, comprehensive budget planning is a must. A project manager can rely on handy estimation tools to ensure the correct funds are allocated over the project lifecycle. Project costs should be continuously monitored and diligently reported to stakeholders for transparency and account-ability.

The process of Cost Management planning involves developing a budget that takes into account potential alterations and methods for monitoring and control-ling expenditures. The cost for each individual task or line item is evaluated to include all the resources necessary for task completion. Combine all the task costs together to generate the project budget. The budget can be adjusted according to earned value analysis.

Earned Value Analysis is a project management process used to measure project performance by comparing the actual cost and work completed against the planned cost and work scheduled. It provides a way to forecast the actual cost and schedule of a project based on its current status and expenditure.

Cost Management functions are processes required to maintain financial control of projects. A project should have cost assessments for project initiation and throughout the lifecycle of the project. The cost management task group creates tools like the Function chart and Function Impact Matrix chart to encompass a project lifecycle's entire cost control strategy. The cost function chart includes functions like cost estimation, budgeting, control, and applications. The functional impact matrix shows the relationship between the cost management function and other project management processes.

Project Quality Management is the procedure of verifying that a project meets the expectations of its stakeholders. The process includes identifying and defining quality standards and detailing how they will be achieved. It includes monitoring and controlling the project to guarantee those defined standards are met. Project Quality Management aims to deliver a product or service that meets or exceeds the customer's requirements while optimizing the use of resources and minimizing waste.

Quality management planning can be a part of the comprehensive project management plan or included in a separate document for quality specifications.

Communications Management

Effective project management relies on strong teamwork, which is fostered through clear and open communication among all members involved in the project. It includes the team itself, stakeholders, and any other parties interested in the project. Communication must be timely and accurate, and consistent. Communication is executed in a predetermined plan. For instance, if an issue were to surface, there need to be plans in place for who to contact and how to appropriately contact them. Communication strategies are evaluated regularly and modified according to the project's needs. Areas to consider:

- Communications plans
- Kick-off meetings
- Conflict resolution
- Communication strategy platform/plan

- Status and progress reports
- Virtual communications
- Templates
- Project websites

Risk Management

Risks are most often predictable events or situations that can lead to positive or negative outcomes in terms of a project's objectives. Through risk assessment analysis, risk is given a probability score. A risk management plan represents a document the project manager prepares to include foreseen risks, an estimation of impacts, and how the team will respond to each risk.

Risk management plans are an essential component of project management that involves identifying, assessing, and managing anything that can come in the way of successfully completing projects. A risk management plan outlines how a project team will identify, analyze, and respond to potential risks, as well as how the stakes will be monitored and controlled throughout the project lifecycle.

Identifying potential risks can be done by reviewing project documents, conducting stakeholder interviews, and using other techniques such as brainstorming or SWOT analysis. Once potential risks are identified, they are assessed based on their likelihood and impact on the project.

After risks are assessed, risk response strategies are developed to address each risk. Risk response strategies can include avoiding the risk, mitigating the risk, transferring the risk, or accepting the risk. The risk management plan should also have contingency plans for high-risk events that cannot be avoided or mitigated.

The risk management plan is then monitored and updated throughout the project to ensure that risks are effectively managed. This involves regular risk assessments and reviews of the risk management plan to ensure its practicality and relevance.

Overall, a well-developed risk management plan is critical to project success. It helps identify potential risks before they become problems and allows project teams to develop effective strategies to address them. By proactively managing risks, project teams can reduce the likelihood of project failures and ensure that projects are completed successfully.

Risk management plans include an assessment matrix. This is a tool to evaluate and prioritize risks depending on how likely they are to happen. The matrix typically consists of a grid with likelihood and impact levels, and each risk is assessed and assigned a score based on its likelihood and impact.

The project team can define the likelihood and impact levels, typically represented by a numerical or color-coded scale.

Procurement Management

The hiring of external personnel like subcontractors is the domain of procurement managers. The manager controls the process, supervises it, and closes the contract after satisfactory work completion. Procuring external help affects the project schedule and the budget. This includes statements of work, terms of reference, proposal requests, and vendor selection (Westland, 2019). Procurement can also involve acquiring essential items for the project in order for the overall project objectives to be met.

The Evolution Of Project Management

It is worth mentioning that we are working in a dynamic specialized field that is evolving rapidly. We as project managers need to be adaptable and flexible to know when traditional approaches are still necessary, and when maybe embracing the new will allow us to adjust and accommodate the way businesses are changing. A good example of the current evolution of the project management space, is the retirement of the

Project Management Body Of Knowledge (PMBOK) 6th edition. For a very long time, the Project Management Institute (PMI) has been established as the industry standard for the common language we call project management. The PMI, is addressing the need to evolve with the new industry standards and keep the project management field up to date and ready for change. With this new PMBOK 7th edition, the PMI has moved away from their more traditional process based approach and has adopted a more flexible approach that allows a project manager to tailor its practices to meet the project and industry needs. The latest guide has a definitive emphasis on the agile and hybrid approach to project management and a new section that is labeled project management principles. In this era of dynamic change, it is crucial to acknowledge that the concepts of the past retains its value. While the evolving landscape demands adaptability, mastering the foundational concepts of the project management field remains essential for every project manager. These enduring principles empower professionals to navigate the ever-changing terrain with confidence and proficiency. Don't forget, knowledge is powerful. The PMBOK guidelines are versatile, making them applicable to all project types, and going forward, learning how to be adaptable will align you with newer modern day project management practices.

PROJECT MANAGEMENT METHODOLOGIES

Project management methodologies are principles and processes used as guidelines to plan, execute, and deal with different aspects of a project. They help the project manager to prioritize tasks and complete the project.

This section aims to explore some of the essential methodologies in project management and provide valuable insights into their application and relevance within the field.

Traditional Project Management

It is the simplest way of managing a project using project management software like Monday.com, Asana, SmartSheet, etc., to establish milestones, plan and organize tasks, and achieve goals. It is a good option for uncomplicated projects and involves describing the project scope, setting a timeline, and forming a budget.

These interdependent factors affect the viability of a project, creating an iron triangle.

Traditional project management comprises five phases, initiation, preparation, execution, monitoring, and closing.

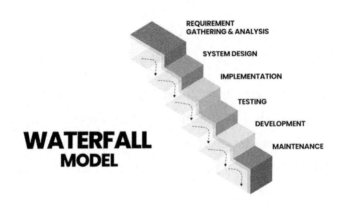

Agile

The principal distinguishing feature between traditional project management and the Agile approach is the flow of time. While in the traditional method, the linearity of the timeline in a project is emphasized, when using Agile, the team can split the project scope into two to eight-week-long phases called sprints. Let us understand the key differences between the traditional and agile methods.

Approach

Traditional project management follows a structured, linear approach that focuses on planning, executing, and monitoring tasks in a sequential manner.

Agile, on the other hand, is iterative and flexible, emphasizing collaboration, continuous improvement, and adapting to changing requirements.

Time management

Traditional project management typically relies on detailed project plans with fixed timelines, whereas Agile favors shorter, iterative timeframes that allow for ongoing testing and adaptation.

Scope management

Traditional project management aims to define the scope of the project at the outset and strictly adhere to it throughout the project's lifecycle. In contrast, Agile embraces change and encourages ongoing collaboration with stakeholders to refine the project's scope as needed.

Team structure

Traditional project management typically involves a hierarchical team structure with clear roles and responsibilities.

Agile, in contrast, promotes a self-organizing team structure that empowers team members to collaborate, communicate, and contribute to the project's success.

Risk management

Traditional project management emphasizes risk avoidance and mitigation, whereas Agile encourages risk-taking and risk management through continuous testing, feedback, and adaptation.

Overall, while both methodologies aim to deliver successful projects, they differ in their approach to project management, time management, scope management, team structure, and risk management.

After each agile sprint, the team draws lessons learned, adjusts the iteration, and changes requirements before beginning. Projects that demand fast delivery, adjustability, operations flexibility, and active client participation are ideal for the Agile technique. Extensive initial planning is unhelpful when using the Agile approach because of its fluid nature. Typically these are small to medium-scale projects. Larger projects are better for traditional methodology. Its dynamic nature is congruous with projects for product delivery or software. In fact, a group of software developers first introduced its manifesto in 2001.

Other than software, projects that are high on ingenuity and fluidity, like computers, medical devices, food, or clothing, are suitable for the Agile method. This method also works well for fast-tracked projects like marketing.

AGILE METHODOLOGY

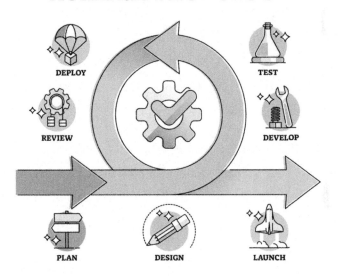

Extreme Programming

Kent Beck designed extreme programming in 1999, which applies to situations that need frequent alterations. Despite its radical name, extreme programming is an extension of Agile software development. It has short project phases (development cycles) and multiple releases, improving efficacy. Extreme programming offers fluidity in project management for clients needing a clear vision of their requirements which evolve into the project.

PRINCE2

PRINCE2 refers to Projects In Controlled Environments. It was designed for IT projects by the UK government in 1989. Its application in general project management occurred later, in 1996. It is popular across the UK and Europe, besides the United Nations. PRINCE2 is gaining popularity in developing economies like India and China.

Unlike other methods, PRINCE2 has seven principles, themes, and procedures rather than a comprehensive methodology applicable to all types of projects. PRINCE2 is suitable for larger projects in the public domain.

The principal features of PRINCE2 are:

- Flexibility
- Organized team structure
- Breaking up of work into manageable and feasible task components
- Product-oriented planning
- Business justification

Since its launching, PRINCE2 has had two significant revisions in 2009 and 2017. PRINCE2 methodology advantages are as follows:

- Superb functionality
- Organized approach
- Ensures maintenance of business needs
- The flexibility of decision-making points
- Maintains effective communication approaches
- Helps in enhancing project management efficiency

Hybrid Methodology

Hybrid project management methodology involves adopting two different project methodologies and combining their various strengthening aspects. The hybrid method, thus created, is a technique to improve project outcomes.

Different combinations of the Waterfall method, Critical Path Method (CPM), Agile, Six Sigma, traditional, or PRINCE2 can produce hybrid methodologies. Typically, combinations of Agile with another procedure, such as the Waterfall approach, will create a hybrid Agile methodology, which has the adaptability of Agile with the traditional sequential Waterfall approach.

In essence, both methods' desirable features are included in the blended technique by circumventing their disadvantages and combining their best aspects. In Agile hybrid methodology, for instance, project planning and a work breakdown structure (WBS) follow a Waterfall method, while the tasks are executed using an Agile method. The Waterfall technology assures the team of the assigned tasks and the broad project scope. Conversely, Agile provides the team with functional flexibility and the ability to review the outcome after each short sprint.

While Agile methodology is celebrated for its adaptability, its rapid and iterative nature can sometimes pose challenges in execution. Hybrid Agile approaches, on the other hand, offer a flexible middle ground that can provide teams with a sense of confidence and ease during transitions and changes.

To successfully implement a traditional/agile hybrid plan, it's important to note that the initial planning and definition stage is done through a traditional approach, while the subsequent execution is done through an agile approach. Poor management of these two methodologies can lead to challenges. A project manager should have a thorough understanding of both methods to avoid issues when implementing hybrid plans.

OTHER METHODOLOGY

Waterfall

The waterfall methodology is a linear approach that has a sequential and structured process. The Waterfall methodology allows the project to progress linearly, where each phase is finished before progression to the next stage. Gantt charts are used for planning and scheduling the Waterfall methodology.

The name Waterfall is apt for the project phases cascading down like a waterfall. Each stage of the project is completed before moving on to the next one.

Scrum

Scrum involves short sprints for project management. The methodology prioritizes adaptability and customer feedback, with an emphasis on delivering value to the customer quickly and frequently. It is most suited for a small cross-functional team not exceeding ten individuals. Typically Scrum has a cycle duration of two weeks of brief regular meetings called daily Scrum meetings, led by the Scrum master.

Scrum methodology is mainly used for software development, although there are claims that it can be applied to other businesses like retail, event management, etc.

Scrum functions within the configuration of the Agile project management method.

This method allows the team to collaborate on complex projects. However, the role of the project manager, also called the Scrum Master, may not be the same as those of traditional project management methodologies. The scrum master manages the scrum team to supervise if they are following the scrum principles, while the job of the PM is broader in other project methodologies.

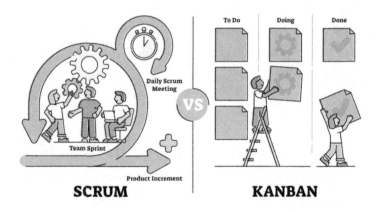

SCRUM | **KANBAN**

Kanban

The Kanban project management methodology is a visual approach to handling the project workflow. Kanban was introduced in the late 1940s by Toyota to their lean manufacturing model called the Toyota production system.

Kanban in Japanese means billboard; all the project-related tasks are placed on a Kanban board to explain the workflow and progress to the team members. It decreases slackness. Agile teams use Kanban boards for storyboarding and planning the arrear tasks in software development. Indeed, Kanban originated in the software industry but found its application across sectors like human resources, marketing, and organizational strategy. Everyone can use the readily accessible Kanban boards to depict the project phases, deadlines, individuals involved, generated ideas, and many more (Westland, 2021).

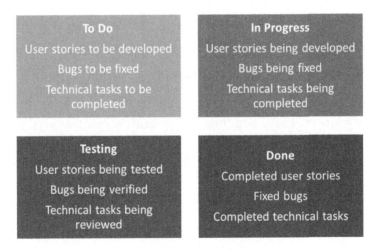

Illustration: Sample Kanban Methodology

Morgan R. Walker of DuPont and James E. Kelley, Jr. of Remington Rand designed the Critical Path Method in the 1950s. DuPont used the method for the Manhattan Project.

The Critical Path Method (CPM) is a project management technique used to identify the activities that are critical to completing a project on time. By identifying the critical path, which is the sequence of activities with the longest total duration, project managers can determine which activities must be completed in a timely manner in order to meet the project's overall deadline. CPM can help project managers maintain the project schedule, allocate resources, and identify potential delays or risks.

Use the CPM method as a tool to construct a comprehensive project model to show the sequence of activities that are critical to the project. In the diagram, all tasks listed in the work breakdown structure, their durations, task dependencies, and milestones representing key project phases or deliverable due dates should be included. Such information helps to determine the project's longest sequence, called the critical path.

CPM is effective for small or mid-level projects, but can also be utilized for larger projects. The volume of load for large projects makes CPM more challenging, and using project management software could be more desirable for them. However, CPM has a proven track record for being a thorough methodology that can provide an enhanced depth of analysis for monitoring the project lifecycle.

HOW TO CHOOSE THE RIGHT METHODOLOGY?

To accommodate the current scenario of a constantly evolving project environment, the project manager has to choose a methodology that needs to be flexible, allowing for the finest performance standards of an organization. The entire project process is then carried out in a clear, compatible, and replicable way following the suitable methodology. The use of methodologies also helps the team gain efficiency and knowledge from the finished projects, building a knowledge base for future reference.

The Project Management Institute defines methodology as the practice system, procedures, and rules individuals use in a discipline. The tenet of project management is: one size does not fit all projects. Each project has its specific requirements with respect to budget, quality, and timeline. Choosing an incorrect methodology may enhance the risks associated with the project.

The assortment of methodologies makes choosing the best suitable for a project complex. People often tend to use the method they are comfortable with (Boehm & Turner, 2004).

An example would be the need felt by software developers to choose a more fluid and fast approach to management methodology instead of the traditional systems in developing their strategy, which inspired other sectors to develop their methods.

Factors that affect the choice of method suitable for particular projects include the following:

- Cost and budget: Determine the budget for the project and account for situations like future risks and cost impacts.
- Size of the team: Consider the number of individuals for the project, including the stakeholders. Whether the team is small and self-organizing that does not require assignment commissioning by the manager regularly or a large team, requiring meticulous delegation is also a point of consideration.
- Overall allowance for creativity: A good project can generate favorable results that will positively impact the whole organization's reputation. Creativity and flexibility are both

important considerations, but always adjust these to what will be best for the project as a whole. If the scope for flexibility is limited, do not forcefully seek it. Typically, research and development projects have more room for creative components.

- Flexibility: Determine the nature of the project scope. Is it adaptable, and will that affect the outcome?
- Timeline: Consider the timeline needed to present the brief, and whether the project needs to be expedited for any reason. Take into account requirements that emphasize a quality product or deliverable over a definite timeline.
- Stakeholder or client cooperation: Ascertain the involvement of the stakeholder or the client in the process and their key roles and responsibilities in the project.

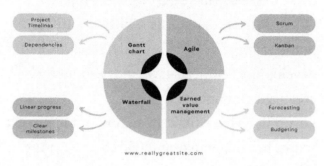

Applicability of the Methodologies

This section will explore the breadth of these methodologies to determine their suitability across various projects.

Waterfall

The Waterfall method is used for several projects like manufacturing and construction projects where any subsequent changes or pivots are difficult. The sequential arrangement of the Waterfall approach is as follows:

- Requirements
- Analysis
- Design
- Construction
- Testing

- Deployment & maintenance

The problem is such an arrangement does not allow room for alterations. The linear arrangement of the project makes it difficult to amend the errors when expectations do not match afterward. As swimming against the waterfall is daunting, going back to the previously completed phases of Waterfall procedures is challenging, to say the least. Hence, using this method is feasible under the following circumstances:

- The project has a clearly defined final goal without any scope for alterations.
- The stakeholders are decisive and definite about their requirements.
- The project is unchanging and well-grounded.
- The organization is regulated, requiring documentation and substantive tracking.
- A project that needs mid-term staff appointments, requiring rapid training and speed maintenance to hold the timeline within limits.

The Waterfall project management methodology may not be the most ideal for these specific scenarios:

- The project needs alterations or has numerous unknown factors.
- The requirements of the project are not clear at the outset. It is possible to have the full parameters only once the project starts.
- The process requires continued testing or adjustments to feedback.

Previously, the Waterfall model was used to develop applications like Customer Relationship Management (CRM) systems, Human Resource Management Systems (HRMS), Supply Chain Management Systems, Inventory Management Systems, or Point of Sales (POS) systems for Retail chains for different enterprises.

Until 2000, the Waterfall model was popularly used in software development, which continued even after the publication of the Agile manifesto in 2001. However, its limitations, like lack of flexibility in operations, led the software projects to switch to agile or hybrid methodologies.

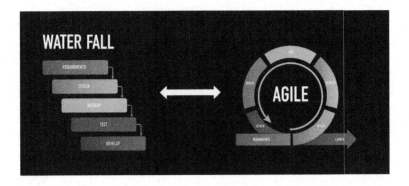

Agile

The limitations of the Waterfall and traditional software development methods led to the development of the Agile project management methodology. The iterative lifecycle model for Agile is more flexible and allows for an evolution of creativity in a step-by-step manner.

The project starts with partial specifications and implements only a part of the project, such as with software, reviewing in stages to plan the requirements for the next step. In essence, the project methods adapt to the different phases of the project requirements.

The Agile method led to different sub-framework and methodologies like Scrum and Kanban. They all have the following standard features.

- Collaborative teamwork
- Fast-tracked method
- Allowing changes according to data

Thus, Agile project management methodologies are best for brief task phases and projects with periodic testing, reevaluation, and adjustment.

Several Agile methods require adding tasks to the project timeline. The project teams resolve them in each phase or cycle after the project manager prioritizes the backlog, enabling them to know what to finish at the earliest.

Agile is suitable for the following purposes:

- The project can change course
- The result is unclear at first
- Speed is more crucial than perfection
- The stakeholders are involved in each project stage

Agile is inadvisable in the following conditions:

- The project requires considerable documentation
- The deliverable is precise and established at the outset
- The project does not support alterations
- Team members are not self-driven
- The project has rigid deadlines that must be fulfilled

Agile methodology is communicative, collaborative, and suitable for most management areas. The Agile approach is versatile and can be applied to managing many areas to increase organization and reduce stress. From small businesses such as restaurants to giant corporations like Apple and Microsoft have adopted Agile methodology to work better and faster. Banking majors like JP Morgan Chase, multinationals like Philip, travel enterprises like Lonely Planet, and even museums like the National Art Museum of the Netherlands have used Agile for innovative projects like developing a business strategy or generating public affinity.

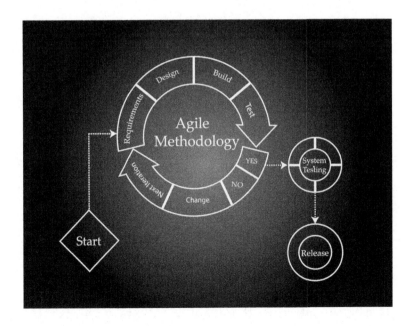

Scrum

Scrum as a framework is suitable if, as a project manager, continuous collaboration and improvement of the work is ideal. However, Scrum entails dedication and cooperation of the whole team.

Kanban

Use the Kanban framework to present a visual representation of the work. With Kanban, it is easy to give an overview of each task's relation to time or milestone. It can be used for project management knowledge domains like content marketing processes or human resource management.

Kanban improves productivity in several ways. It is possible to perceive the impasses leading to project risk. For instance, columns in the Kanban board represent specific activities combined to generate the workflow. If one of the columns is clogged, one may re-examine the particular stage of the process for errors or backlog that must be cleared.

Project managers can limit the number of works in progress using Kanban work-in-progress (WIP) limits. WIP allows only a certain number of tasks in each column at a time and uncovers the bottlenecks in the workflow, alerting the team members to finish the backlog promptly before working on other tasks in the queue.

Kanban is helpful in the following areas of project management:

- The project entails a visual representation of the project's progress
- To provide glimpses of status updates
- WIP limits motivate the team to stay on course
- The project manager or owner prefers to work using a pull system. The kanban pull system is a Lean manufacturing technique. It functions to produce a task or a product that the customer has specifically requested. This eliminates waste, as the supply is made on a demand basis and not on assumptions.
- The pull system of kanban favors the implementation of WIP and works best with self-driven team members, who may make adjustments as required by the customer.

However, Kanban does not work well in the following areas:

- The project is a complicated process with a large number of stages

- The project uses a push system of management that is not dependent on demand
- The products are produced and marketed to potential consumers in a push system, which works with some manufacturing companies. Project managers use the push approach to work based on the assumption that the product will be received by the end-user or customer.

Extreme Programming

Extreme programming demands dedicated teamwork from all concerned members of the project. It has a well-defined set of rules based on five values: straight-forwardness, communication (especially in-person interactions), feedback, integrity or respect, and courage.

Use extreme programming in the following circumstances of project management:

- Teamwork and collaboration are valued and desired
- The project has a small and co-located team

Extreme programming is not ideal for projects with members in different time zones and countries.

Critical Path Methodology

The Critical Path Method (CPM), or Critical Path Analysis, identifies and schedules the vital tasks of the project and their dependencies. The milestones in the path designate the completion of a set of functions or phases, enabling the staff to move on to the next phase.

The critical path can be visually expressed through flow graphs or Gantt charts.

The Critical Path Method is applicable in the following project situations:

- For a significantly complex process
- A project with a large number of dependencies
- A project which requires a visual representation of the sequence of the tasks

- A project with stringent criteria like planning and deadlines
- The project manager and the team support and prefer working with algorithms
- The project manager must identify the vital tasks for the appropriate distribution of resources

Critical Chain Project Management (CCPM) is an extension of CPM that considers the human factors of the project, like errors, backlog, or resources. By including buffers in the critical path, it allows for the flexibility in the CP to address anything that could derail the progress of the project.

However, the Critical path method is not for simple, straightforward projects with variable timelines and has little room for alterations.

The traditional methods resist alterations and emphasize compliance with the plan as a metric for success. Thus, they lean heavily on process and documentation.

Agile and its related methods are more dynamic to changing environments and project requirements. These methods were developed to undertake changes. Their approaches are value-based instead of premised on plans. Heavy documentation is replaced by explicit team understanding, knowledge, and collaboration.

Agile is more work-oriented and does not rely on theoretical knowledge garnered via certifications like the PMP. The practical nuances one learns in the course of passing and getting these certifications (time management, calculated guesswork, compartmentalization, and so on), however, are always a bonus.

PRINCE2

Usage of the term "In Controlled Environments" suggests the conventional nature of PRINCE2 in *prescribing* the principles, themes, processes, tasks, and rules of project management to be aimed toward the result. It is formal and structured, with some flexibility in the later versions. It offers a flexible and scalable framework that can be tailored to suit projects of various sizes and complexities. PRINCE2 is based on best practices and lessons learned from numerous successful projects. This methodology has a heavy emphasis on project governance, with a clear focus on roles and responsibilities to provide business justification throughout the projects lifecyle. Management in stages is key with Prince2.

These features may be useful while selecting a suitable methodology for a project:

- Use a heavier methodology for a larger group.

- For a critical system, apply a methodology that focuses on improving visibility and transparency.
- However, note that a slight increase in methodology size or density increases the project cost significantly.
- A face-to-face communication strategy is the most effective mode of communication for sharing ideas (Cockburn, 2000). Group meetings on whiteboards are better than sharing documents online.

ROLES OF DIFFERENT TEAM MEMBERS IN A PROJECT LIFECYCLE

Projects progress through a structured arrangement called The Project Lifecycle. Similar to the human lifecycle, it has a beginning and an end. In the intervening period, various activities progress, bringing the project to fruition. It is imperative that a project cannot continue for an indefinite period because the tenet of the project is to produce results. Hence, all projects, from vehicle design to developing software, pass through lifecycles. Naturally, lifecycles are characterized by various activities conducted by multiple project participants. Their roles will be discussed in further detail in this section of the book.

Stakeholders

Stakeholders are individuals or organizations with an active interest in the project who can also be investors. The project result has a direct bearing on their interest. For instance, the client can be the main stakeholder in a book editing and publication project.

When one considers stakeholders, always leave room for human error and feedback. Especially when it comes to larger or more complex projects, stakeholder interests can be varied and, at times, may not match because of the heterogeneous nature of a group. Key roles of the stakeholders can change during the project lifecycle and can escalate or diminish concerning the phase of the project lifecycle. As a project manager, one must be calm when navigating variations in these interests while maintaining reasonable boundaries of expectations.

Stakeholder satisfaction is crucial to the project's success, and the project manager's job is to keep them informed, engaged, and onboard during the project lifecycle. Depending on the resource requirements for a project, the types of stakeholders can be external or internal.

Cost Team

Cost is one of the three iron triads of a project, along with time and project scope, that can affect the lifecycle adversely. A project manager has the responsibility of ensuring allocated budgets are spent well and for the intended purpose. Most projects will have a cost team to take the burden from the project manager's shoulders.

Depending on the size and scope of the project, the cost team will frequently be made of subject matter specialists who will work collaboratively with the project manager to keep them up to speed on the project finance, budget, and cost implications. The budget must be managed to leverage maximum advantages and reduce expenditure and wastage. Project cost designation requires an understanding of the types of costs.

Costs can be direct, including labor, materials, tools, and equipment. Direct costs are typically one-time expenditures fulfilled by the project funding or the department.

Indirect costs or overhead expenses refer to features not identified with a project function or activity but are nonetheless required for proper project functioning. They include rent, utilities, administrative expenses like travel, costs for the accounting department, personnel department, salaries, quality control, etc.

The next step is crucial because it determines if the project will receive the green light and involves cost estimation to identify the resources needed to complete the project within its scope. The project manager has a crucial role in preparing the budget based on the cost estimation document. Finance team members can work with the PM to supply an accurate budget or cost estimations. If some areas require more funding, the project manager must identify the risks and apportion the budget to make appropriate changes. Cost estimates depend on the following factors:

- Labor
- Materials and equipment
- Utilities
- Vendors
- Risk

Project Logistics

Project logistics involve planning, execution, and supervision. Logistics is the comprehensive management of resources for acquisition, storage, and transportation. This may mean transporting cargo or materials to the project site or supplying the deliverables to the end users and customers.

Logistics in military connotation means generating, stowing, and transporting supplies and equipment. Nowadays, logistics is essential for numerous businesses like retail and manufacturing that require handling and transferring resources across supply chains. Logistics may also include locating potential distributors and suppliers in order to carry out project tasks. Poor logistics affect the entire supply chain and will negatively impact businesses, which is why this is such an important field of expertise.

As logisticians, relevant tasks are:

- Efficient and accurate evaluation of supply chain data
- Ensuring timely and secure delivery of goods
- Optimizing logistics processes
- Ensuring compliance with regulations in their field

The success story of Amazon reflects the ingenuity of business approaches and efficient logistics of the supply chain.

Logistics is a complex operation that undergoes a feasibility analysis before accepting an assignment. For example, projects requiring the shipment of heavy cargo to a destination require considering different transportation systems, such as road, rail, ships, or airplanes, and different terrains and logistics constraints. The project manager has to address different aspects of logistical planning like customs brokerage and obtaining customs clearance as an example. International shipments involve complex issues like monetary transactions, embargoes, and other specifications (What Is Project Logistics, 2022).

However, project logistics include the following characteristics:

- Converging: to bring the materials or equipment to the project site.
- Temporary: an example like on construction projects where the project supply chain is temporary in nature.
- Customized: each project has customized supply requirements specific to each project.

The components of project logistics are as follows:

- Bulk items in logistics are defined as standardized goods that have basic specifications and don't require rigorous quality control measures before delivery.

- Commodities are generalized items for the project but require a proper quality check.
- Modular Plant Units are prefabricated structures and may be required for specific projects like building construction.
- Process Equipment includes tools required for the project. These have specifications and quality checks and may ask for a site visit to decide suitability for the project requirements.
- Customized and Costly Items require rigorous quality control.

Aspects of logistics include inventory, supply chain, and transportation management.

Using logistics software can address many logistics elements. Typically businesses have their own supply chain and logistics departments, and will have subject matter experts to assign to project teams for logistics support. The use of software systems can be very helpful to the overall logistics management for projects. Areas software is useful for logistics are:

- Warehouse and distribution solutions that manage the daily operations of a warehouse.
- Fleet management software to manage all information on fleet and assets throughout the project lifecycle.

- Order management software for entering, processing, and fulfilling orders and other related activities like purchases, payments, and deliveries.

Project Engineers

Project engineers handle most of the technical aspects of a project and are a must throughout the lifecycle of engineering or technological projects. Manufacturing businesses, software, and research and development industries typically need project engineers to communicate expectations, objectives and needs to all stakeholders in order to achieve the specified project goals. The project engineer may play a major role alongside the project manager in the project's budget, planning, and team member selection to meet the standards of the project's specialized technical requirements. Some of their work areas are as follows:

- Monitor safety and legal requirements of the project site
- Appraisal of project proposals and plans to form project objectives
- Determine project phases and requirements
- Determine project specifications after thoroughly inspecting performance standards, customer requirements, and product designs

- Gather and analyze project information to produce status reports and propose future actions
- Design and initiate testing methods to supervise the project grade
- Plan and supervise engineering tasks
- Prepare drawings for design and construction
- Propose policy and procedural regulations to maintain project integrity
- Manage a team of engineers on the project

The nature of work for a project engineer can vary depending on the project type and industry. Some aspects of projects with specialized needs may comprise the following:

- A technical project where the project engineer manages the specialized engineering team of the project.
- Project design is a crucial aspect of technical project planning, which may need an iterative methodology, and is the domain of the project engineer.
- Requirement analysis is developed based on stakeholder and end-user expectations.

- Process improvement addresses the points of process breakdown, helping to reduce errors and promoting efficiency.
- Computer-aided design (CAD) is used for precise designing or modifications per requirements.
- Niche problem-solving skills can help settle issues like identifying areas where team members require assistance, conflict resolution, or intricate design and technical problems.
- A technically complex project where mistakes can be expensive for the organization will require project engineering support.
- Mathematical skills are essential, particularly in-depth knowledge of trigonometry and calculus, which help in solving problems, designing products of features, and analyzing the results.
- Engineering innovation concerning creativity, problem resolution, and resourcefulness helps to achieve excellence for a technical project (Simplilearn, 2023).

COMPETITIVE ADVANTAGE

In project management, competitive advantage refers to the distinctive capabilities and resources that a project team has at its disposal, which allow it to complete projects more efficiently, effectively, or economically than its competitors. The following example will illustrate strategic planning for a project and how ingenuity and resourceful project management can give businesses a competitive advantage. This example concerns the famous and quintessentially American vehicle company Ford and the first generation of Taurus cars.

Ford launched the first generation of Ford Taurus cars in the late 1980s. The inception of the project was in 1980 and was completed in 1986. Ford established a new set of project management and development practices, maintaining a close association with vendors and subcontractors. The project mantra was cooperation and harmony; customers embraced the Ford Taurus, and the business generated profit. Yet, the project manager was dismissed for delaying the project by six months.

Ford was heavily counting on the success of its Taurus model to hit back at the popular Japanese car models which saturated the market. It wanted to repeat the success of the first generation of Taurus the subsequent time. The second generation of Taurus started in the early 1990s and was finished in 1995, earlier than the first generations, taking five years' time.

The project manager approached the project schedule with a sense of caution. While he remained dedicated to following it diligently, he may have inadvertently overlooked other critical aspects of the project, such as building and maintaining strong vendor relationships, promoting team collaboration, and ensuring high product quality. In prioritizing the timeline, he may have missed valuable opportunities to enhance the project's overall success and sustainability.

The project was a debacle, and Ford could not duplicate the magic of its first-generation cars.

This example highlights the difference between a project managed according to strict protocol or operations, and those managed more strategically. In some instances like above, it can spell the difference between success and failure.

Strategically managed ventures focus on the quality of results and the job, while operational businesses are only concerned about finishing the job without ensuring its quality. This difference can affect future business prospects for an organization (Shenhar, 2000).

SWOT analysis can improve success in the long run and give projects a competitive edge. It is a practical, data-based, factual representation of the project's strengths, deficiencies, risks, and options. The findings are usually collated to form a unified objective. Relying on assumptions or beliefs for project management is not effective, and a clear data-driven approach is better suited for success. The project manager uses the SWOT analysis as a guide to manage the project.

Strengths

The strengths of a project give it an edge in competition. Typically it refers to internal characteristics of a project that are identifiable and controllable. Some examples of project strengths are team member expertise, experience, dedicated software, or transparency of operations.

Weaknesses

Weaknesses are also internal factors that must be addressed to ensure success. Some examples can be new employees or resource overallocation in one particular area (which can jeopardize work in other areas), making it impossible to finish the assignment within the timeframe of the schedule. Other weaknesses can be a lack of transparency, deficient funding, and stakeholder non-involvement. Some of these problems can be resolved, like resource overallocation, which can be managed by reassigning tasks, spreading out resources, and bringing in other resources.

Opportunities

Opportunities are external to the project and can help deliver project success. Opportunities can be pre-existing or more likely to occur in the future. An example could be earlier project completion or saving resources.

Threats

Threats are external factors that may pose a risk to the overall success of the project. Threats can be things like weather conditions, the rising cost of material or equipment, or bankruptcy. Like opportunities, threats can be real or perceived and require management accordingly.

THE SWOT ANALYSIS

The strengths, weaknesses, opportunities, and threats analysis framework is used for evaluating the competitive ranking of a business, which helps in strategizing and planning different business-related activities, including projects. SWOT is also termed situational assessment or situational analysis. It is applied in the initial decision-making process to locate the internal and external factors which can benefit or hinder the project objectives. Users of SWOT ask questions to obtain helpful information in each category of the project, determining the competitive advantage.

SWOT Table

The SWOT table visually represents the internal and external factors affecting a project. The internal factors are arranged in the top row, and the external factors are on the bottom rows of the table. Items on the left side of the table benefit the project, while those on the right are more alarming.

To do a SWOT analysis, consider the following aspects:

- Engage all the stakeholders in the project's process: the team members, sponsors, financiers, owners, and customers in order to identify potential areas for improvement and develop effective strategies for success.
- Promote a group thinking session(s) with all stakeholders to enumerate the factors of each of the four categories of a SWOT list.
- Arrange the factors in the list according to their impact on the project performance.
- Create the SWOT list and distribute it among all members of the project. A SWOT list should be placed in a location for easy referencing by all stakeholders if necessary.

- Assess present opportunities and threats concerning the project. Make action plans to deal with factors that can be controlled, improved, or removed.
- Make prospective plans to consider future opportunities or threats. It must include *how* to know the opportunity or the threat has arisen and the *method of action* to address them.
- The list must be reviewed and evaluated frequently to accommodate new factors or alterations (Everitt, 2022).

Below is a visual representation of a SWOT table. Questions are written down on possible suggestions to identify the task priorities. The list can be done on a whiteboard or a sticky note session.

Strengths

1. What are the competitive advantages?
2. What are the resources?
3. Which products are doing well?

Weaknesses

1. What are areas for improvement?
2. Which products are underachieving?
3. What resources are lacking?

Opportunities

1. Which new technologies could benefit the project?
2. Can there be testing of new areas?

Threats

1. Which regulation changes can affect the project?
2. What could our competitors be planning?

IMPACT OF PROJECT PHASES ON PROJECT OUTCOME

Each phase plays a crucial role in project performance, and none can be sacrificed for the other. A project manager must go through all the phases meticulously, involving the stakeholders skillfully and perceptively.

Initiation Phase

The project is defined in the initiation phase, clearly establishing its identity. Its scope, resources, and goals are established. The team's responsibilities are decided, and stakeholder interests are clarified. There must be a clear vision of what to expect from the project, which is decided during project initiation.

The initiation phase emphasizes the following project aspects.

- The necessity of the project or its benefits is ascertained through a project charter or business charter for the larger projects. The *project charter* provides the project's goals, aims, scope, budget outline, and team members concerned with the project. Conversely, a *business case* includes an overview of financial analysis and an estimate of the return on investment (ROI) of the project. A business case provides project risks, a risk management plan, an action plan on decision-making, and a communication plan if the project is approved.
- The relevance of the resources asked for.
- Identification of project stakeholders who would approve, provide resources, and impact the project in various ways. A project stakeholder analysis ensures everything has been evaluated and nothing is omitted by arranging the stakeholders into four categories according to their impact and interest in the project. Stakeholder *buy-in* or active engagement also enhances transparency and prevents expensive barriers from stalling the project in later phases.

- A feasibility study for large projects ensures project completion within the resources available.
- Team formation with the right talents and experiences for the project. The team structure is formed and contractors are identified. Use the RACI chart to define the roles and responsibilities of team members.
- One will need the right infrastructure and tools for the project (Macneil, 2022).

Tools to utilize in the planning phase are things like a *project proposal*: a document defining the project and sketching the crucial dates, requirements, and goals. It helps to secure stakeholder involvement, funding, and allocation of resources for the project. Two additional tools for the project's initiation phase are a *project charter*: an official document describing the project and the principal factors for realizing the project goal, and a *RACI chart*: a graph that plots team member roles and responsibilities.

Planning Phase

How to do a project is the domain of project planning. It is characterized by hectic activities such as setting budgets, timelines, and milestones, as well as gathering materials and documents. Risk management, installing change processes or change management, and chalking out communication protocols are all within the ambit of the planning phase. The list of crucial activities during the planning phase are as follows:

- Develop milestones that effectively work toward project completion
- Construct a schedule for tasks and milestones, highlighting time estimates and likely time buffers
- Install change processes
- Decide the mode and frequency of team member and stakeholder communication
- Create and sign vital documents such as non-disclosure agreements (NDAs) or requests for proposals (RFPs)
- Create a risk register for risk evaluation and analysis.
- Give a kick-off meeting to commence a project

Tools for planning can include a *Gantt chart*: a horizontal bar chart members can use to visualize the order and timeline of each task. The other is the *risk register*: a chart showing the probability, effect, and mitigation plans for risks connected to the project.

Execution Phase

Execution is the time to be in action, arguably the most critical phase of the project. In this phase, all the work comes together to carry out the project plan. A poorly planned project will have problems with executing the project goals. Specific activities in this phase are as follows:

- Use tools like Gantt or burndown charts to monitor task progression
- Mitigate risks that arise during the phase
- Keep informing the stakeholders about the project progress
- Manage alterations in the change requests

Tools for execution can include change requests, documents to propose changes to a project's scope or objectives, and a burndown chart, a graphical work representation to show the amount of work completed in a sprint and the remaining time (4 Phases of the Project Management Lifecycle Explained, 2022).

Monitoring And Control

The Monitoring and Control phase is a critical component of project management. Here are some key activities that typically occur during this phase:

- Monitor project progress to ensure it's on track, within scope, schedule, and budget constraints
- Identify project risks and issues, and implement appropriate mitigation strategies
- Review project plans to address changes in scope, schedule, or budget
- Manage project resources to ensure they are being used effectively and efficiently
- Conduct regular status meetings with the project team and stakeholders to communicate progress and address concerns
- Perform quality control to ensure that deliverables meet standards
- Conduct testing and verification activities to validate that project objectives have been met
- Prepare project reports to communicate progress to stakeholders

The Monitoring/Control phase is an important part of a project because it enables the project team to:

- Ensure delivery per the agreed scope, schedule, and budget
- Manage and mitigate risks to minimize their impact on the project.

- Improve project processes and outcomes by identifying areas for improvement.
- Provide stakeholders with updates on project progress, and risks

By monitoring and controlling the project throughout its lifecycle, the project team can increase the likelihood of success.

Closing Phase

In this phase, the project activities culminate, the finished product or the service is handed over to the customer or client, and a final evaluation of the project lifecycle provides lessons learned.

Some activities during the closing phase might be:

- Conduct a retrospective analysis to identify areas for improvement and opportunities for future enhancements and document lessons learned
- Communicate project closure to the stakeholders and provide an impact report
- Review all project deliverables and ensure they are complete and accurate
- Release project resources to include team members, equipment, facilities, and excess budget

- Create a project closeout report

Some useful tools for the closing phase are an *impact report*: a compilation of metrics to show the project's impact. Another tool is a *project closeout report*: a summary of project performance and achievements with learning points for future reference. A *closeout report* is another tool that documents the project's achievements and challenges.

SUMMARY

Here are some things to remember from this chapter.

- Make robust project objectives using the SMART criteria.
- There are different project management methodologies.
- Use traditional project management for well-defined linear projects. Use Agile project management for projects that require flexibility.
- Traditional project management comprises five phases, initiation, preparation, execution, monitoring, and closing.

The next chapter will cover the five stages of project control and how they relate to the project plan.

3

THE PLAN

This chapter discusses the project plan as an arrangement and sequence of documents explaining how the project should be conducted or executed and the five phases of project control. PRINCE2 describes the project plan as a statement that mentions how the project will be done and when the objectives will be attained, indicated by the products, milestones, activities, and resources used.

The project plan includes risk, resource management, and communication strategies and provides a layout of scope, costs, and schedules.

A plan is the best way to start the risk management process. A plan gives a clear roadmap for the project and is pivotal in successful project management.

Having a well-defined plan is crucial for project managers in order to navigate the complexities and uncertainties of a project and ensure they deliver successful execution of the project. The plan breaks down the tasks into manageable portions to maintain a well-organized workflow that can be efficiently supervised.

CREATE A PLAN TO MAKE THE PROJECT SUCCESSFUL

A project plan, also called a work plan, is a strategy that includes the project objectives, goals, and tasks which must be done within the allocated resources and deadline to deliver a quality product or service.

A project plan is the same as a *work plan*. Both provide comprehensive activities to meet the project objectives.

A *project charter* differs from a plan; it is typically created *before* a project plan. A project charter is a *basic outline* of the plan and contains objectives, scope, and responsibilities. The plan is created after the project charter is sanctioned and is more comprehensive than the charter.

Agile frameworks are usually operated with Scrum and sprint methodologies, which are iterative. Still, like others, the Agile team works better with a project plan in place.

The benefits of a project plan can be the following:

- Improving work organization
- Determining the roles and accountability of the project team
- Providing a basic schedule to all stakeholders
- Assuring resource availability *before* commencing the project
- Identifying and predicting areas of potential challenges, allowing the project team to proactively address them during the planning phase
- Modifications to the project plan
- Ensuring project viability and helping to generate success
- Improving team efficiency and project outcomes or deliverables

Write a Professional Project Plan

Creating a project plan is the project manager's responsibility; to do it, use project tracking tools to monitor data and the project initiatives. Devise a practical and purposeful work plan. All work plans comprise the following features:

- Goals and project objectives: Project objectives and goals provide answers to *"why"* the project is being done. The team members know that they are working *toward* the organization's goals, which keeps them motivated. A clear and precise emphasis on goals and objectives in the plan links them to the tasks, making them realistic instead of abstract concepts. Write *SMART goals* to measure project success and to understand *how* the project *follows* the business objectives. *Project objectives* should account for the *specific deliverables* that the project will produce at the end. Finally, be sure to establish metrics for success (Martins, 2022).
- Stakeholders and their roles: Decide which individuals will work on the project and their respective roles. It gives them clarity concerning the individual roles on the project and removes confusion. Use a RACI chart to identify the approvers for the project, the frontrunners, the contributors, and individuals who must remain aware of the project's progress.
- Scope and budget: A project plan that mentions a budget is a well-thought-out endeavor. Budget-making requires a clear concept of the different requirements for the project and

shows the project manager's competency. Determine the nature of resources that the project will require, like equipment, materials, human resources, and budget. Estimate the cost of each line item and task to prepare a cost baseline. Add management reserve (MR) to the cost baseline to complete the project budget. An MR is a budget for "known-unknown" or unplanned occurrences. The project manager is authorized to use it for management control purposes.

- Milestones, deliverables, and project dependencies: Project milestones show the completion of a group of tasks or "when" a new phase starts. They do not set dates, but achieving them has considerable meaning for the project and the team. Project dependencies also express "when" to start work, for instance, after completing the preceding tasks. Use a Gantt chart to clarify project dependencies.

- Timeline and team assignment: Timelines help with task prioritization and meeting deadlines. Larger projects with variable dates work well using a project roadmap. It explains the work orders without fixing precise dates. Address the significant tasks and responsibilities first. Then use a work plan template to break the project into smaller components, including all the specifications. Next, allocate the start and finish date for each task and subtask. Enlist all necessary stakeholders and the respective team roles they're involved in. A cohesive project timeline visually represents all these features.

- Communication strategy: Communication keeps everyone aware of the project activities and progress, including roadblocks. Consider the purpose and frequency of project-specific meetings, managing and sharing status updates, and the tools required.

- Preparing a project schedule: A project schedule includes all the tasks required to reach the final result. Break the schedule into phases, and set milestones depicting the end of one phase and the beginning of the other.

- Conducting a risk analysis: The project plan should be flexible to accommodate internal or external risks that affect the project's triple constraints. While creating the plan, include a procedure to follow project progress during the execution phase by using status reports and risk monitoring procedures.

WHY PROJECT PLANS ARE CRUCIAL TO PROJECT SUCCESS?

The project plan is the roadmap for two vital project phases: execution and monitoring/control. The plan includes all relevant information like goals, objectives, resources, schedules, milestones, timelines, and risks. All of these elements are essential functions for a successful project, which the project manager uses to supervise and control.

Since the project plan contains the budget necessary for project resources, the team functions optimally to maintain project costs within the allocated budget. The timeline and milestones enable the team members to understand how the budgetary constraints are affected by the progress through the schedule.

Careful team assignment sets responsibilities for the project roles, ensuring the designated individual is available for their tasks. Good communication channels keep all the stakeholders abreast of project progress or hurdles. Team members can work more efficiently and effectively with thorough project planning in place.

A flexible plan accommodates change requests by addressing them as required and provides a mitigation plan for risk management. Distinct goals and objectives and effective communication concerning risks also guarantee product quality and customer satisfaction. Above all, the project plan maintains the transparency of decisions and actions related to the project.

It contains the following:

- Project scope statement
- Risk management plan
- Change management plan
- Cost management plan
- Resource management plan
- Stakeholder management plan
- Quality plan

HOW TO START A PROJECT PLAN?

A project plan essentially summarizes all conceivable aspects of a project. Although the project managers ultimately create it, they need the participation of the project team and key stakeholders through meetings, workshops, or surveys.

Various project planning tools are available to facilitate the design of project plans., some of which are described in the following section.

Project Planning Techniques: Using Visualization Tools

Some project planning techniques are as follows:

- Brainstorming: This tool uses the collaborative knowledge and expertise of the project team to obtain the entire project perspective. Brainstorming sessions are creative and open, and the collective knowledge can be immensely helpful in identifying project risks or other issues. People who find it comfortable to work with templates may find lateral thinking challenging. Still, the project manager can use it to design a plan.
- Critical path analysis: Use it for projects with multiple interdependent and simultaneous tasks. It ascertains if some tasks can run concurrently. The analysis will determine the sequence and significance of tasks by outlining the most effective path and which areas require more resources. It involves three steps: 1) place all tasks on the project timeline, 2) ascertain which tasks can run jointly, and 3) identify task dependencies
- Work breakdown structure: To prioritize tasks within the project scope, the use of a work breakdown structure (WBS) can be

advantageous. WBS is often compared to a puzzle piece, where the tasks are pieces arranged to create the bigger picture. To utilize the WBS tool, break the project into phases, identify the milestones between each phase, and plan the tasks in each milestone. WBS helps create a statement of work.

- Gantt chart: Utilizing a Gantt chart as an outline for your project can help keep your tasks organized and on track. Start by uploading your task list and naming the columns with the tasks on the left-hand side of the chart. Then, add start and finish dates on the right-hand side columns to create a timeline for each task. By linking interdependent tasks, you can ensure team members are aware of task dependencies and keep the project functioning smoothly. Gantt charts can be used throughout all project phases, aiding in task assignments and keeping the project on schedule.

- Cause-and-effect diagram: The cause-and-effect diagram, also called an Ishikawa or fishbone diagram, was designed by Kaoru Ishikawa, a Japanese organizational theorist, to show events have causes. Things can happen and build over the course of a project. Timely intervention can help resolve the issues faster and more efficiently.

The cause-and-effect diagram has a central backbone. Bones from this main structure represent significant events like legal issues, new technology, etc. that could affect the project's outcome. Smaller bones emerge from these side bones to support a visual perspective of the cause and its effects. Use the diagram to address any such issues in brainstorming sessions or meetings.

- PERT: The Progam evaluation and review technique (PERT) tool assesses project time. Assessing project time through the PERT tool is crucial for effective project management, as time impacts resource utilization, deliverable production, and overall project outcomes. Finishing a project is a prerequisite for starting a new one, even if it builds upon aspects of the previous project.

PERT is an effective tool for creating precise and efficient project schedules, including start and finish dates, milestones, and a clear mapping of task dependencies by breaking them into smaller components.

Each task receives a time-to-complete approximation like Optimistic (O) for the fastest, Most likely (M) for the required deadline, and Pessimistic (P) for the most time-consuming tasks. E, for the estimated time, is derived by statistical calculations to obtain the project variance (Vs). The variance determines if the project is on time, needs to catch up, or is ahead of scheduled time.

- SMART goals: SMART ensures that the goals are *specific, measurable, achievable, reliable, and time-bound*. All these criteria are vital to achieving a successful project, and planning them even before starting a project is recommended.

SMART
OBJECTIVES

RACI
MATRIX

KPI

AGGREGATE PLANNING

Aggregate planning is most suitable for businesses requiring consistent production of goods or services. The emphasis is on generating an overall management plan ensuring streamlined and non-stop production, typically for 3-18 months, to meet the projected deadlines within the allotted project budget.

ROLLING WAVE PLANNING

Rolling wave planning is a project planning technique that involves continuously planning and executing short-term phases of a project while maintaining a long-term plan for the overall project. This technique allows for adjustments to be made as the project progresses based on the knowledge gained during the previous phases, which can improve the precision of the project plan. Rolling wave planning is particularly useful for complex or uncertain projects, as it affords flexibility and adjustment to the variable nature of the project.

PROJECT ROADMAP

The project roadmap is a *visual tracking tool* that is generated using Gantt charts. It is applied to plot the tasks, milestones, and deliverables on the timeline, helping the project team understand the exhaustive project plan. It is valuable *throughout the project duration*, and some of its advantages are as follows:

- Overview of the bigger project plan, identifying the key stakeholders, and their roles
- Brief explanation of project phases, goals, and objectives
- Provides vital information on scope, risks, and resource management
- Supports communication with all stakeholders

Project roadmaps become an invaluable component of the management portfolio if the project manager has several projects running concurrently (Keup, 2022).

A *product roadmap* has specifications for developing the products instead of projects and is suitable for a product development team.

Since it's impossible to predict every variable at the start of a project, employing certain methods can help mitigate difficulties arising from unforeseeable circumstances. One such method is incorporating project assumptions, which serve as contingencies within the project plan. By assuming the documented features are accurate at the time of planning, project managers can create plans in the best interest of the project. For instance, including an assumption that requested resources will be appropriate can safeguard the project manager in the event that the customer requires future specifications.

Discovery Phase (Week 1-2)
- Identify project stakeholders and gather requirements
- Conduct user research and create user personas
- Determine technical specifications and constraints

Design Phase (Week 3-4)
- Develop wireframes and visual design concepts
- Create a functional prototype
- Obtain feedback from stakeholders and make necessary revisions

Development Phase (Week 5-10)
- Build the application in sprints using Agile methodology
- Conduct regular testing and debugging
- Deploy the application to a staging environment for user acceptance testing

Deployment Phase (Week 11-12)
- Finalize testing and debugging
- Deploy the application to production environment
- Conduct final user acceptance testing

Post-Launch Phase (Week 13-16)
- Monitor and maintain the application
- Gather feedback from users and make necessary improvements
- Plan for future updates and enhancements

Infographic: Sample Project Roadmap

PLANS ARE CRUCIAL IN MANAGING PROJECT RISKS

Poorly executed risk management can lead to project failure, often as a result of reactive measures and conflicts that could have been avoided with effective risk management strategies integrated into the planning phase. By proactively addressing risks before they manifest, projects are better equipped to overcome potential obstacles and ensure successful outcomes.

Effective risk management serves the organization and its projects rather than the customers and requires proactive planning by the project manager to develop risk mitigation strategies, allocate resources, and budget for remedial actions. Implementing contingency plans preventatively in the project plan is far more effective than pulling from reserved resources or an established budget once the project is underway. This approach allows project managers to proactively address potential risks, ensuring the project remains on track and successfully achieves its goals.

To establish a clear set of project objectives, it's essential to first assess the organization's ultimate goals and interpret them in the context of the project. Additionally, it's important to consider external factors that could impact the project's timeline, such as future regulations. Perhaps most importantly, it's crucial to assess the organization's risk threshold or tolerance to ensure the project is appropriately aligned with its overall risk management strategy.

Consult with professionals, like Subject Matter Experts (SME) involved in similar projects within the organization, to understand the nature of the risks. All stakeholders should be aware of the project's risks and their mitigation plans to expedite remedial methods.

Effective risk management is essential for successful project outcomes, as risks can cause delays, resource overruns, and financial losses. In order to mitigate risks, it's crucial to allocate resources proactively during the planning phase and schedule activities that manage potential issues. Additionally, documenting the processes and tasks used to control risks is essential for effective risk management. The level, type, and transparency of risk management should align with the project's significance to the business to ensure that risks are adequately managed and that the project aligns with the organization's broader risk management strategy. Define the risk categories, tracking methods, risk reporting methods, and mitigation strategies for different degrees of risk probability and their effects on the project's outcome (Jersak, 2022).

Take time in the planning phase to make the project a winner.

SUMMARY

Here is a recap of the essentials from this chapter.

- A project plan is the most important document designed during the planning phase.
- The plan is a strategy for project execution and monitoring that includes the project objectives, goals, and tasks, which must be done within the resources and deadline to deliver a quality product or service.
- The project roadmap is a visual tracking tool that is generated using Gantt charts.

- The project roadmap is applied to plot the tasks, milestones, and deliverables on the timeline.

The next chapter will discuss the project manager's tasks and responsibilities in order to better comprehend their roles during the third phase of the project cycle.

4

LET'S EXECUTE

This chapter will discuss the activities and responsibilities of the project manager to give a better understanding of their roles during the project execution or implementation, which is the third phase of the project lifecycle.

It is the stage of action and gives shape to the outlines of the project plan. The strategies described in the planning phase are adopted to finish the tasks systematically and according to the project sequence mentioned in the plan.

This phase is challenging and exciting because of its dynamic nature. The project manager must manage the progress of the project schedules, costs, and tasks while keeping the team members motivated and engaged to keep the project moving toward a successful close.

A fundamental aspect is managing the communication network, which plays a crucial role in keeping all stakeholders informed of the project status. It prevents bottlenecks and unnecessary delays. Incomplete tasks that are not prioritized or managed within a given timeframe can accumulate and create bottlenecks in the project workflow, ultimately hindering the progress of the project. These roadblocks can slow down the pace of the project and impede its successful completion.

The execution phase of a project is the means by which a business or organization achieves its ultimate goals. The purpose of this phase is to do the work described and defined in the plan to meet the project objectives. The clients and the stakeholders obtain the deliverables made during this phase which is usually the lengthiest and the most exacting of all project phases. During this phase, the principal roles of the project manager include the following:

- Managing staff and key stakeholders
- Managing the processes, resources, and costs
- Managing communication with all stakeholders

THE STEPS OF EXECUTION

Project Scope Execution

The project scope is defined, and its requirements are established after careful research during the planning phase. It contains a work breakdown structure, which is executed in this phase, ensuring effective and optimal resource and time utilization to reach the milestones. Any unexpected delays or situations can be handled by planning a realistic timeline that allows contingency measures.

Manage Scope Creep Proactively

Scope creep is different from a *scope change*. Scope change is an official action following a formally accepted request for change. Scope creep refers to uncontrolled and unauthorized changes or additions to the project's original scope, objectives, and require-ments. When the customer and the project manager officially recognize change requests, the budget, time-lines, and resources can be amended accordingly, and the changes requested can be proactively managed. Thus, in scope creep, deadlines and budgets are not adjusted according to the scope creep, and the changes are not predetermined.

PMI's definition of project scope helps to understand scope creep. The scope of a project is the size of what the project will deliver and the work required for it. Thus, scope creep is a subtle shift from the original scope due to adding or changing new and existing features. One way it can happen is by accepting a minor change, followed by another.

Hence, the project scope must be well-defined during the planning phase to prevent unnecessary troubles for the organization and the customers. For instance, with the Chrysler PT Cruiser, how the car would be timely delivered to the dealers after launching the product was not established, leading to delays and customer dissatisfaction.

Handle things professionally and methodically from day one to proactively address scope creep. Key stakeholders must be involved in the plan, and stakeholders can provide a project charter enlisting their aspirations from the project. Understanding their vision avoids misaligned project understanding and a poorly defined project objective, which occurs when the client's expectations and the team's understanding of the scope do not match.

Other methods are prioritizing tasks, using technology, charging for requests, and rejecting requests that do not benefit the project (What is Scope Creep and How to Avoid it in Project, 2022).

Team Management

Team management includes:

- Assigning tasks to the team members
- Supervising their work
- Motivating the project team and ensuring productivity
- Troubleshooting any bottlenecks that may arise due to scope creep

Address Changes

Use the change control processes established during the planning phase to address change requests to project scope. Changes can be approved or dismissed based on predetermined criteria, including project goals and objectives, schedule, and budget in the change control process.

Stakeholder Communication

Communicate with the stakeholders based on the frequency and mode they wish to receive the updates. Keep the stakeholders informed of the status, changes, and any unfortunate problems or setbacks occurring on the project. By ensuring a transparent and clear picture of the state of the project, the project manager can avoid numerous pitfalls while managing the project gambit.

Acknowledge Achievements

Recognizing the hard work and dedication of a team is crucial in building a positive work environment. When a team has accomplished a milestone, it is important to acknowledge their efforts and show appreciation for their work. This can be achieved by hosting a celebratory event, which not only serves as a way to recognize the achievement but also fosters a sense of camaraderie and teamwork. By taking the time to celebrate, the team's morale and motivation will increase, leading to even greater success in future projects.

Team Meetings

Establishing a consistent channel of communication with stakeholders is vital to ensure transparency and facilitate project success. Holding regular meetings provides an opportunity to update stakeholders on project progress and discuss ongoing activities.

Through these meetings, status reports can be generated and valuable feedback can be exchanged, allowing for adjustments to be made in a timely manner. By fostering open lines of communication, stakeholders will feel involved and invested in the project's success, ultimately leading to better outcomes.

Track Project Progress

In order to ensure the success of any project, it is important to track its progress at every stage. By doing so, project managers can ascertain whether the work is meeting the project's objectives and goals. Having measurable goals and objectives established from the beginning, will make this process easier and more effective.

These measurable goals and objectives provide a clear roadmap for the project team to follow, ensuring that everyone is working towards the same targets. They also provide a framework for evaluating progress, allowing project managers to evaluate whether the project is on track or if adjustments need to be made.

Regularly tracking progress against measurable goals and objectives also helps to identify potential issues or roadblocks early on in the project, giving the project team more time to address any issues that may arise.

Documentation of Changes

Projects are most often complex and dynamic, and changes are to be expected throughout the project's lifecycle. It is important to promptly identify areas that require modification and resolve them in a timely manner to avoid potential delays or overruns. To ensure that changes are properly documented, it is essential to record the actions taken to modify the project. By doing so, project managers can maintain control over the project's progress and ensure that any changes made are aligned with the project's objectives and goals. Documentation saves time and resources for similar future problems (Caietti, 2022).

STRATEGIES THAT HELP PROJECT EXECUTION

Empower The Team

Great team leaders are empathic and know the abilities of their team members. Entrust tasks to team members in their areas of expertise. By delegating repetitive tasks to others, project managers can demonstrate trust and confidence in their team's abilities while freeing up time to focus on more critical tasks.

Assess risks as an ongoing process and provide the team with contingency plans. Enable the team to make decisions and take the initiative to enhance processes that will benefit the project's goals and objectives.

Assigning specific tasks to team members does not mean relinquishing control of the project or abdicating personal responsibilities as the project manager. Instead, it provides an opportunity to empower and enable the project team to execute tasks. This demonstrates the project manager's trust and respect for their contributions and decisions. By fostering a spirit of camaraderie, tension can be reduced while cooperation is encouraged, ultimately leading to greater success for the project as a whole.

Use brainstorming sessions to welcome new ideas and consider their usefulness regarding the project's purpose. The team appreciates the acknowledgment, and in turn, improves group involvement and cohesion.

COMMUNICATION

Effective communication is critical to the success of any project, as it promotes transparency and ensures that decisions and actions are made with the project's best interests in mind. By implementing strong communication strategies during the planning phase, project managers can ensure that everyone involved in the project is on the same page and working towards the same goals. This level of communication enables teams to work more efficiently and make more informed decisions, ultimately resulting in greater productivity and better outcomes.

Thus, establish stable and reliable communication channels *during the planning phase* and set a robust communication network to prevent project setbacks.

Executing Communication Strategies

Good communication strategies are important in all project phases. Below are some common communication strategies worth incorporating:

Use the Plan

- Engage dedicated staff to convey information at all stages. The project communication plan states how vital information must be communicated to relevant stakeholders and team members.
- Use project collaboration tools for sharing documents and feedback and tracking project status and a communications management workflow or chain stating how and with whom information obtained is shared.

Manage Communication Strategy

- In order to maximize the benefits of a project, it is important to use the information generated from each phase and apply it to the subsequent phases, allowing for a continuous improvement process.

- Discover the weaknesses in communication strategies and resolve them promptly.
- Supervise the communication strategy as part of monitoring to identify functional and sluggish areas that require attention.
- Identify the *project objective* concerning the relevant information before sending it to the internal staff and external stakeholders. It ensures that the recipients can address it and close the loop.
- To ensure stakeholders take appropriate action based on project information, it's important to present it in a clear and precise manner, avoiding jargon and technical language. This is especially crucial as not all stakeholders may have the requisite technical knowledge to fully understand the project. Additionally, stakeholders must be aware of the information's source and significance to make informed decisions.
- The communication channels for the stakeholders must be clearly defined for a project. A project that specifies only e-mails as a communication channel may have difficulty communicating in an *emergency* (The

Importance of Communication in Project Management, 2023).

USING DIFFERENT PROJECT MANAGEMENT METHODOLOGIES

Traditional

The traditional methodology or the Waterfall technique is suitable for the following project conditions:

- Large project teams working on complex projects
- Straightforward projects requiring fewer new technologies
- Projects necessitating precise and strict documentation
- The project requires all deliverables at once during the project closure.

Thus, construction projects where the entire project is a single sequence, and the project's success is determined by finishing the deliverables within the deadline and below budget are suitable for traditional methodologies.

Traditional project management implies systematic adherence to the project plan having precise requirements, and clarity on the nature of final deliverables. The entire project runs seamlessly from start to finish, following the linear arrangement of the project phases: initiation, planning, execution, monitoring, and closure. For larger and structured projects, its benefits are as follows:

- It has well-described team roles and responsibilities, ensuring the best use of customized resources.
- Total completion of the deliverables at the end, thus, closing the project.
- The project's linear model is conducive to establishing focused and precise expectations with team members and stakeholders (Montgomery, 2021).
- Documentation is exhaustive and accurate in order to meet requisite compliance, regulatory or otherwise.
- The project withstands stakeholder monitoring and compliance audits, ensuring financial stability.

Hybrid

Get the flexibility to accommodate changes by using hybrid methodologies like Agile or Scrum with the Waterfall technique. The hybrid framework utilizes the best of traditional and modern to help progress and complete successive sprints. It gradually unfolds the bigger picture in a more step-by-step style of creation. A close link with the clients ensures product acceptance at the end of the project.

The hybrid model draws on the linearity of the Waterfall, its five phases, planning and primary requirements, and the iterative sprints of Agile, the quality assurance (QA), and deployment.

The project team can enjoy the adaptability to create an image of the bigger picture and divide it into fragments. While reassembling, the components are broken into smaller sections to make the tasks more manageable for execution.

The hybrid model allows for team cooperation and communication, favors reviews, and promotes timely status report updates to the stakeholders because of more frequent sprint tracking reports. Thus, project risks are reduced. The project is categorized into smaller work packages to allow better solutions to problems arising during execution.

If client input is crucial for agreeing with the product or solution throughout the project, the Agile or Scrum mode of execution and test phases can provide that. The traditional model adopted in the beginning upholds stakeholder collaboration to define and rectify the majority of the requirements for the product; the rest evolves during the iterative sprint phases of execution, which can be based on project scope and priorities.

Agile

The agile lifecycle is designed to be iterative and incremental, allowing for a process of continuous learning and optimization in an environment characterized by high levels of change and uncertainty in requirements. Incremental development ensures the creation of deliverables in a step-by-step manner.

The Agile methodology identifies and breaks down the work types into tasks requiring less than a day to finish. Work is completed in iterations or sprints of two to four weeks, with the shorter duration being suitable for teams with less experience. Careful task evaluation helps in deciding the number of tasks for a sprint.

A prioritized task backlog is created to ensure the completion of project phases. Execute items from the work backlog, prioritizing tasks before each sprint. Retrospective scrutiny after executing a sprint helps understand supportive actions for the project and areas that can be improved. Use Agile project-specific completion metrics to modify the plan of the next sprint phases accordingly.

KEY PERFORMANCE INDICATORS (KPI)

Key Performance Indicators or KPIs are metrics used to measure the project's performance against its goals. Three main elements are measurability, team performance, and aligning KPIs with organizational goals, which involves carefully selecting goals prior to choosing KPIs.

Uses of KPI

- Indicators of performance
- Accurate indicators of the effectiveness of the process to generate the deliverables
- They answer most of the stakeholders' questions regarding the project
- Empower the staff members and enable them to gain experience from the specific information.

How to Identify KPI?

- KPI must be linked to objectives and goals
- Must represent the organization's criteria for success or failure
- They must be justifiable and resolvable

- Must have long and short-term implications
- Must represent stakeholder requirements and interests
- Must reflect crucial project features
- Must represent project performance
- Must set targets and track progress

KPI Types

Process KPIs are used to measure the effectiveness of a process, for instance, delivering deadlines.

Input KPIs determine the resources used in a project and assess value, and it is important to measure factors such as the quality and quantity of materials.

Output KPIs measure the deliverables, for instance, the quality or quantity of a product or service.

Leading KPIs are used to measure progress towards a specific goal or objective that is predictive of future success. Leading KPIs are prospective and help organizations identify potential issues before they arise.

Lagging KPIs is a metric used to measure performance after an event has occurred. Most financial KPIs are lagging KPIs, measuring the results of past activities.

Outcome KPIs, also known as results-based KPIs, are metrics that measure the actual results or outcomes achieved on a project or process. The focus is typically on the end result of a process rather than the activities that contributed to the end result.

Qualitative KPIs are metrics that are measured subjectively, based on non-numeric or non-quantifiable data. These KPIs are typically used to evaluate performance in areas that are not easily quantifiable, such as customer satisfaction, brand reputation, or employee morale.

Quantitative KPIs are the most common performance metrics that are measured objectively using numerical or quantitative data. These KPIs are typically used to evaluate performance in areas that are easily quantifiable, such as revenue, sales, or production.

Some good KPIs include the following features:

- Associated with project and business goals
- Determined by the management
- Clearly defined metrics
- The Key Success Factors (KSF) only change with a major change in business strategy.
- KPI must change with the fulfillment of objectives or change in management perspectives.
- KPIs must be SMART, specific, measurable, achievable, reliable, result-focused, and

relevant, besides being time-bound (Wootton, 2020).

Some Examples of KPI in Project Management

- Cumulative Flow (Kanban)
- Project schedule (Agile or Waterfall)
- Problems seen in code review
- Problems discovered by Quality Assurance
- Problems encountered by customers

SUMMARY

Here is a quick summary of what was covered in this chapter:

- Project scope is executed in the project execution phase.
- It is crucial to monitor scope creep and address issues promptly to prevent project delays.
- Team empowerment helps in work efficiency and motivation.
- Different methodologies can be used depending on the nature of the project.

The next chapter will examine the project monitoring phase, which is essential for tracking progress, identifying issues, and taking corrective action. Project monitoring and control ensure that the project achieves its goals within the given time, budget, and quality constraints.

5

PROJECT MONITORING AND CONTROL

The project monitoring and control phase runs parallel to the project execution phase. Effective management of project work and performance is crucial to ensure that performance remains aligned with the project's goals and objectives. Otherwise, it may cost resources and strain the budget.

The management activities during this phase are project-specific and typically involve actively reviewing the project's status as it progresses, assessing potential issues and risks. During this phase, the project manager will proactively initiate any necessary changes or corrective actions required. Thus, the responsibilities of the project manager during the fourth phase of the project's lifecycle involve:

- Monitoring progress to remain within the schedule
- Keeping within the budget
- Preventing scope creep
- Handling risks

The project manager needs real-time feedback on the project's performance in order to conduct assessments of a project's current status. This phase essentially becomes a *vital process* in avoiding commonly occurring mistakes like scope creep or outlying tasks still needing to be completed.

Making decisions based on solid data rather than assumptions is essential to identifying and mitigating risks on every project. While previous approaches may have been effective in similar settings, it's important to recognize that each project is unique and requires individualized management strategies.

In the realm of project management, monitoring and controlling are distinct activities. Monitoring is focused on data collection and analysis while controlling focuses on these evaluations to proactively initiate necessary changes in order to keep the project on track.

Insufficient monitoring can impede the ability to properly identify a problem, leaving it unresolved and potentially derailing the project. Thus, setting appropriate controls can help more effective task delegation among team members. Plans are essential in providing a roadmap to indicate the general direction of project progress. However, performance tracking is an important component of monitoring and control.

PROJECT CONTROL

The process of data collection and analysis in a project to maintain the cost and schedules are called project controls.

Project controls are an essential part of project management and focus on two key elements: cost and schedule. Their aim is to minimize any deviations from the original plan by providing data-driven insights on resource utilization within the set timeframe. Essentially, project controls act as a safeguard for the project management team, allowing them to focus on delivering the required outcomes.

Project control plays a key monitoring role, providing assessments and recommendations that impact the project manager's decision-making. This ensures that the necessary remedial actions are taken to keep the project on track and deliver the desired outcomes on time.

Project controls, therefore, involve all functions of the project lifecycle. They help to measure project status, predict outcomes, and enhance performance in deficient areas.

It addresses the following areas:

- Schedule management
- Scope management
- Quality management
- Risk management
- Time management
- Resource management

The essential components of the project control process involve the following aspects:

- Scheduling: Project control starts with a project schedule detailing tasks and assignments and the time required to complete them. A Gantt chart can be used to highlight the tasks and critical dates along the timeline and schedule.
- Costs: A cost management plan is used to optimize resources within the project cost. The estimated costs and financial risks to the project are assessed.

- Risk: A risk control plan assesses project risks and their overall impact on the project objectives.
- Performance: Project controls identify baseline deviations of performance and allow the opportunity to correct them.
- Communication: In order to keep the project team focused and provide valuable information to stakeholders, it is essential to maintain clear and consistent communication about the preparation and reporting of project status updates throughout the entire project lifecycle.

The project control cycle involves the following stages and begins after the WBS is set into action:

- Setting standards for performance baselines.
- Measuring performance through collected data.
- Data analysis compares performance to the reference baselines to locate variances and their causes.
- The variances are corrected to maintain the project budget and deadlines.

Project control methods are clear-cut and reproducible. There are specific project control methods to address different functions, some of which are as follows:

- **Project Charter**: The project charter provides the crucial components of the project precisely and clearly.
- **Responsible, Accountable, Consulted, Informed (RACI) Matrix**: Each task within a project requires one or more individuals to assume specific roles and responsibilities. To efficiently allocate these duties, a RACI matrix is used, which is a responsibility assignment diagram that links task assignments with corresponding roles based on four key factors:
- Responsible
- Accountable
- Consulted
- Informed

The chart indicates tasks, activities, responsibilities, accountability, and decision-making roles supporting the work process and providing definite expectations concerning team participation.

- Work Breakdown Structure: As the WBS aligns with project objectives, it provides a comprehensive estimate of the expenses involved in completing the necessary activities. In turn, the Cost Breakdown Structure effectively indicates the costs associated with each WBS element.

- Critical Path Method: The critical path method is used to identify the longest sequence of activities that must be completed on time to complete the project.
- Project Milestones: A *project milestone* is a precise point in the project lifecycle denoting essential dates, such as the start, end, review, and deliverable due dates (Eby, 2021).

Work Breakdown Structure

The PMBOK guide Third Edition describes WBS as a *hierarchical decomposition* or breakdown of project scope to be enacted by the team to achieve the objectives and produce the necessary deliverables. Although it is a part of the traditional methodology, WBS can be applied to other models like iterative, adaptive, or hybrid methods. It is connected to different estimations like cost, earned value, time, resources, risk identification, and schedule development.

The hierarchical structure of a WBS is a visual representation and can be depicted in different forms, like a tree, table, or graph. The topmost level is Level 1, containing the finished products or services, continuing downward to Level 4, with the primary work packages and deliverables related to the finished products or services.

Each component is numbered for WBS identification and is called a WBS code. The WBS code is included in the WBS dictionary with details on each WBS element.

Fragmenting the scope produces work packages and deliverables, which are documented and measurable products, services, or results created by the team.

A work package consists of tasks not shown in the WBS because it is included in the schedule. Sometimes planning packages in the WBS structure are used to represent outlying work not tied directly to a specific task group. At the top of the work package level, there is a control account that provides management control and oversight.

With WBS in place, problems can be easily identified, and project progress can be assessed and controlled. Team members do not feel daunted by the enormity of the project as the entire project is broken down into structured compartments of a work-to-do list.

After setting the WBS, monitoring, and process control can proceed as follows:

- Execute the plan
- Get the results

- Analyze the results
- Spot the variances to analyze their outcomes
- Acceptable variances are further monitored
- The unacceptable variances are studied for the root cause to determine the options available for modification
- Implement corrective actions
- The results are evaluated further
- Conduct lessons learned

ESSENTIAL FEATURES OF PROJECT MONITORING AND CONTROL

The following features help to track performance concerning the project budget, schedule, and scope:

- Key Performance Indicators: KPIs are indicators to keep the project on track and to align performance to project deliverables within the stipulated deadline and budget. Different data on timelines, budgets, and quality are used to make decisions, initiate changes, and seize opportunities.
- Change Request Monitoring: Project performance data measurement and analysis indicate if the project is on track or requires changes. Submit a change request for projects

that have deviated from the baseline. Once approved, the changes can be implemented to rectify the problems.

- Monitoring Project Scope: All changes made to the project scope must be checked and documented. All relevant documents, like the scope statement and work breakdown structure, must be updated. The project manager must monitor if factors like cost and timeline need any adjustments. Effective project monitoring and control often involve reassessing and adapting the strategy as needed..

- Risk Identification and Control: Risk identification and control is an ongoing process and occurs throughout the lifecycle of the project.

- Effective Communication: Communication is effective when it is timely, relevant, and open. The project manager leads communication with the stakeholders and negotiates for the benefit of the project.

METHODS OF IMPLEMENTATION OF PROJECT MONITORING AND CONTROL

The following functions help in implementing monitoring and control strategies:

- Monitoring project parameters
- Monitoring stakeholder involvement
- Risk monitoring methods
- Using project performance trackers
- Rectifying actions to control project progress
- Managing data documentation

PROJECT PARAMETERS

Set up baseline parameters to closely follow the three project constraints: scope, time, and cost. Choose parameters that include success benchmarks. Project managers use KPIs to track schedule, cost, and performance in order to maintain the project's objectives and standards.

STAKEHOLDER INVOLVEMENT AND COMMUNICATION CONTROL

Project managers must lead the communication with stakeholders. Communicate directly with stakeholders about situations like change requests and explain their effects on the triple constraints to remove conflicts. The project manager may also need to monitor stakeholder disputes to make valuable project decisions.

Implement effective monitoring methods to ensure regular communication with key stakeholders in order to keep them informed of the project's progress.

Using technology for communication can be an effective solution, particularly for larger projects or projects conducted mainly on virtual platforms.

Information sharing with stakeholders, asking questions, and making requests can be done through teleconferencing, e-mails, virtual meetings, or a collaboration site. Brainstorming sessions to resolve problems or extending the project scope may require a virtual meeting or collaboration sites, like a collaboration portal.

Collaboration portals can be used for exchanging status reports, project schedules, documentation, making inquiries, or logging concerns regarding the project.

They can also provide access to the directories of team members.

Some tools that support team collaboration and team communication are as follows:

- Project war or control room
- Project display wall
- Project collaboration wall
- Project flight status board
- 3D Project environments
- Project gamification

RISK MONITORING AND CONTROL

Risk in project management consists of three types: financial, strategic, and performance. Financial risks relate to budget overruns and funding problems. Strategic risks arise from external factors that impact project objectives. Performance risks involve quality, schedule, and technical issues that can affect project outcomes.

Just as there are risks, there is also a way to mitigate them. This is known as a risk management plan. This is a document outlining the strategies, procedures, and resources needed to identify, assess, and mitigate risks in a project. It includes a risk management framework, risk assessment criteria, and a risk response plan to address potential threats proactively and effectively.

The first step is risk identification, which starts with defining the risk in simple terms that feel personable. The means to identify something often becomes clearer when it resonates on a personal level. Risk identification is an early event in the project's lifecycle after determining the requirements, milestones, and timeline.

Risk management can be a challenging time for project managers as they may receive a large number of risk predictions from team members or stakeholders. Remember, it is important not to panic. Understanding that the project or team is not under attack and utilizing effective communication can help to avoid costly mistakes and significantly increase the chances of success.

Participating in or facilitating cross-functional sessions can help teams learn from professionals with diverse experiences and expertise. These teams consist of individuals from various levels and functions within an organization who work together to achieve a common goal. Through cross-functional collaboration, team members can develop a shared language and understanding of the project's various functions and their effects. This can foster effective communication and collaboration by enabling team members to better comprehend and interpret each other's ideas and perspectives.

The next step is risk assessment, where the risk items are evaluated against the Risk Assessment Criteria. The risk identifier can pinpoint the risk on a risk priority matrix to define it.

As part of risk response planning, the two crucial activities include determining the risk response strategy and a plan to implement the strategies. Some response strategies can be as follows:

- Avoidance/Elimination: involves executing a different approach to avoid or eliminate the risk.
- Transfer: Risk transfer is the process of shifting risk management responsibility to another party, like an insurance company or third-party vendor, that is better equipped to handle the risk. For instance, a company can purchase a cyber insurance policy to transfer the risk of a potential cyber attack. In case of a cyber attack, the company can file a claim with the insurance company to cover the damages. Risk transfer is a useful strategy when the risk is too high or

significant for the organization to manage independently.

- Mitigation: involves creating a plan to diminish the chances of the risk or its outcomes.
- Acceptance: involves accepting the risk and coping with it once it happens.

Some risks may need several strategies to mitigate their occurrence or outcomes. Risk response strategies are dynamic and can evolve according to the developing needs or circumstances of the project or business.

During project execution, the risk response plan involves determining triggers, work, roles, schedule, and funding related to identified risks. Risk triggers prompt action and can be specific situations, past dates, or spotted threats that require immediate resolution. Risk triggers not only indicate the presence of risks but also when they are resolved or no longer valid, making them useful for documentation purposes.

Risk monitoring and control require supervising occurrences of risk triggers and launching the risk response plan when needed. Any changes that are likely to produce and generate consequences are supervised. All information is tracked, documented, and reported to assess the consistency of the response plan. The activities can be outlined as follows:

- Identify and track risks
- Monitor risk triggers
- Apply mitigation plans as needed
- Respond appropriately when new risks occur
- Measure the efficacy of the risk management program to enhance it

Inputs for risk identification should include project management and risk management plans, work performance data and reports, as well as project requirements, which are crucial in identifying potential risks

Some crucial inputs are as follows:

Risk Register

The project manager creates the document during the risk identification and updates it as part of the continuation plan. It enlists details like known risks, probabilities, impacts, and triggers.

Risk Report

It gives a quick picture of the risks spotted, responses made, and the likely impact on the budget, deliverables, and deadline. It mentions the persons responsible for controlling the risk implementation and the mutually decided strategy.

Risk-related data and performance reports include the following

- Earned value (EV)
- Planned value (PV)
- Schedule variance (SV)
- Cost variance (CV)
- Estimate at completion (EAC)
- Estimate to complete (ETC)
- To complete performance index (TCPI)

Track and report risk management procedures using simple matrices that catch all the features associated with each risk item, including risk definition, probability, outcome, response, trigger, etc. The worksheets allow for screening and sorting the risk items.

As part of ongoing risk management, it is crucial to periodically reevaluate identified risks. This process generates data that can be used to conduct further risk audits, with the frequency of these audits being dependent on the size of the project. When conducting risk assessments, it is important to consider input from performance analysis in terms of project milestones and deliverables.

Regularly monitoring remaining costs and schedule reserves is important after risk mitigation procedures.

If the reserves are low, the project manager may need to prepare better preventive measures or request a timeline or budget extension. Utilize stakeholder meetings to discuss risks and revise strategies as necessary. Monitoring work performance, along with overall project data, helps evaluate risk planning and execution processes.

Other documents that need regular reviewing include the following;

- Assumption log: assumptions concerning the project risks can change after learning more about associated project risks. Using the log to estimate the likelihood and impact of different risks can provide invaluable project data.
- Risk register: log and record any new information regarding project risks.
- Technical documents: Technical documents must reflect changes made to any technical approaches required to produce the project deliverables.
- Organizational process assets (OPAs) include project plans, risk response plans, lessons learned, policies and procedures, performance reports, other documents, templates, and guidelines (How to Monitor Risk in Project Management, 2022).

Developing a risk program summary based on the Risk Index Priority Matrix structure for reporting gives a clear and straightforward assessment of risk status and the number of risk items still open. Depending on the business or project's specific criteria, the matrix can indicate the risk item's impact in color, such as Red, Yellow, or Green. The color codes help in drawing the summary (Becker, 2004).

The summary should include all the risk items and the project status. This will make tracking the status of risks easier to manage. The use of visual aids, like graphs or charts, can help to represent various aspects of open risks to evaluate the risk status reports.

After assessing corrective or preventive measures, project managers can present change requests before the Change Control Board or management in response to current project risk.

Use the project plan as the baseline to control the progress and monitor any project changes. Monitoring and control continue until the project enters the closing phase.

INTERNAL AUDIT

PARAMETERS TO TRACK PROJECT PROGRESS

Project Scope

Project scope may evolve during the project lifecycle, as is common in many types of projects.

If the project requires an increase in scope, it must be acknowledged, accepted, and approved as necessary resources, funding, and time will be impacted. If not, recurrent scope creep can derail the project.

Project scope is best tracked by *work breakdown structure* with the following features:

- Determines all project requirements
- Splits requirements into smaller deliverables and milestones
- Identifies tasks and crucial resources to achieve deliverables
- Evaluates the time to complete each task
- Defines the critical path

Use *Gantt charts* as visual aids to help the team and stakeholders with project assessments. By providing a clear project timeline laid out on a calendar, all stakeholders can better understand the project scope and methods for executing precise requirements within the allocated budget and timeframe. Gantt charts also help the project manager to track performance and alignment with the project goals.

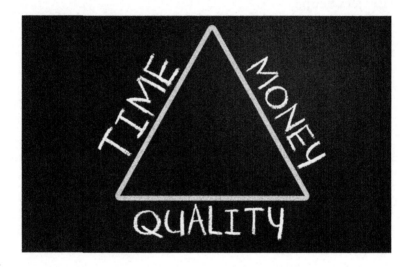

Schedule

The schedule includes the timeline, any project deadlines, crucial milestones, and task due dates. In order to prevent scheduling delays, the project manager must provide slack time as a scheduling buffer. Slack time (also known as float time) is in reference to the amount of time a task or activity can be delayed without adversely affecting the project completion date or the start date of subsequent tasks. Tracking the schedule is an essential part of project monitoring for any project.

Use Gantt charts to track project schedules and KPIs like the following:

- Percentage of tasks completed
- Behind schedule tasks
- Skipped milestones
- Schedule performance index: Earned value (EV) / planned value (PV)

Resource

The project scope identifies the tasks and resources required for a project through *resource forecasting*.

Resources are then *allocated* according to the tasks and requirements.

For problems concerning scheduling or over-allocation, the *resource leveling* technique helps in the appropriate assignment of tasks. It aims to schedule tasks by assessing available resources and task dependencies to prevent overallocation or schedule postponement due to a lack of resources.

Use Gantt charts, workload dashboards, and timesheets to track resource allocation and level workload.

Regular monitoring of resource utilization is necessary to manage scheduling and costs. This helps adjust project plans, schedules, or budgets accordingly while improving project visibility and risk management. Various methods can be used to calculate resource utilization to prevent overuse of resources and enhance ROI. Some useful calculations:

- Utilization Rate Formula: to assess the profitability of resource utilization

Utilization rate = Total billable hours / Total available hours

- Capacity Utilization Rate for the entire team = Total of all employees utilization rates / Total number of employees

- Optimal Utilization Rate Formula

Optimal Utilization Rate = Resource costs + Overhead costs + Profit margin / Capacity utilization rate

- The ideal utilization rate is next calculated, which is the rate that will be charged to the customer (Landau, 2023).

Use slack or float without affecting the critical path to delay the less urgent tasks to complete the project within the available resources and time, called resource smoothing.

Budget

Cost management monitoring involves meticulous planning to include all areas of expenditure like raw materials, layout, etc. Besides estimating individual costs for each item, keeping provisions for contingency is a must. Budget is linked to other success measures like the schedule or customer satisfaction (O'Loughlin, 2018).

Effective budget tracking entails the use of automated tools like specialized databases to assess and predict future costs. KPIs specific for tracking budget may include the following:

- Planned value
- Actual cost
- Earned value
- Cost performance index: Earned value (EV) / actual cost (AC)

VISUAL MANAGEMENT TOOLS

The project monitoring and control phase is demanding and exhausting for the project manager. Visual tools like timelines, Kanban boards, and calendars help reduce work-related stress and improve efficiency. Use them to keep organization and control over all the many pieces of the project that are being monitored. Besides being automated, the benefits of visually managing the project can be as follows:

- Rapid interpretation of information from project status, metrics, and tasks and how they align with the overall project goals.
- Access to information reduces the chances of bottlenecks and avoidable delays.
- Ability to Supervise and monitor the entire project lifecycle.
- Improved team and cross-functional collaboration.
- Allowing the executive stakeholders and team leadership access to status updates.
- Early detection of project dependencies, milestones, and risks to work progress.

The three most popular visual project management tools are:

1. Timelines or Gantt charts
2. Kanban boards
3. Project calendars

They function best in project management software. The formats can be customized, and automated tools can be added to them to tailor to the specific needs and requirements of individual projects.

Timelines and Gantt Charts

If a project demands time as a crucial factor and deadlines as a marker of success, using timelines or Gantt charts can be most helpful. They display when to begin a task and the time required to accomplish the task. Mapping the tasks on the project timeline helps to better allocate and utilize resources in order to evaluate and detect task dependencies early on in the project lifecycle.

One can organize the details of the project in a bar chart to show the relationship between tasks or requirements with time. Gantt charts are great visual tools that are best used in planning, tracking, and communicating the requirements of a project. Keep it simple; a good bar chart will show stakeholders and team members a quick and easy snapshot of project progress and task relationships.

Kanban Boards

Use Kanban boards for projects with multiple daily tasks or flexible due dates. A Kanban board is a visual tool where a card shows each task. The cards are then arranged in several columns depicting the project stages, the individual responsible for the task, task priority, and other related features. When a task or a piece of the deliverable is completed, the card representing it is moved from column to column to track its progress (Thai, 2023).

Thus, Kanban boards are helpful for projects with several stages involving tasks moving from one stage to another and can be used while working with sprints, agile, and daily standup meetings, work requests, scrum boards, etc.

KANBAN BOARD

Stories	To Do	In Progress	Testing	Done

Project Calendars

Calendars can help manage several tasks with different due dates. It works like calendar schedules with milestones, due dates, and records when specific tasks must be started and accomplished.

Data Visualization

Reports or status updates are perfectly suited to be displayed using visual templates. The usefulness of visual aids in planning, tracking, and controlling the project lifecycle has made the job of the project manager a little more manageable. The feedback obtained from using these tools serves as valuable input for analytical work, such as identifying causal relationships, correlations between data sets, and trends, among others.

Some standard tools utilized in Data Visualization are:

- Charts
- Drawings
- Graphs
- Tables
- Pictograms
- Ideograms
- Data plots
- Diagrams
- Schematics
- Technical Drawings or Illustrations
- Maps or Cartograms

Visual thinking is how human minds receive, process, and interpret what is seen. In project management, visual thinking tools utilize this capability to understand complex projects and the immensity of assorted data. Visual tools help develop ideas and a common language for the project team. Why try and manage a project without the extra help from a visual tool? Today, the life of a project manager is stressful enough.

PROJECT REPORTING

The project manager has to collect, encapsulate, and report KPIs to project sponsors and main stakeholders who depend on quality reporting to evaluate progress and performance. The project manager describes how the scope and deliverables align with the project objectives and goals in the report (Williams, 2015).

While conventionally, most reporting was written or oral; the current trend is to use efficient visual methods for project reporting and status updates. Some of the visual tools for the purpose are as follows:

- Earned Value Analysis
- Dashboards
- Kanban Boards (Lean)
- Scrum Boards (Agile)
- Burn Down charts
- Road maps
- Infographics

- Tolerance-Limited EVA charts

SUMMARY

The essential points covered in this chapter include the following:

- The monitoring phase involves checking the project parameters.
- Stakeholder involvement and communication are vital to this phase.
- Risk monitoring methods are crucial to keep the project on track.
- Using visual tools and visual thinking tools can help the project manager to monitor the phase.
- Preparing project reports is essential to evaluate project progress.

The next chapter will discuss the closing phase of a project, which is the final stage. At this point, the project deliverables are completed, tested, and accepted by the stakeholders. It involves formalizing the project completion, releasing resources, closing contracts, and documenting lessons learned.

6

CLOSING PHASE

As the project enters its final phase, the project manager's responsibilities remain significant. Their main focus is to complete all remaining activities and deliverables and obtain stakeholders' verification of acceptance. This involves managing various tasks such as obtaining signatures, conducting payments, and securing approvals while reviewing performance metrics, schedules, and cost constraints against the plan.

FEATURES OF THE CLOSING PHASE

During this stage, all deliverables are concluded and officially handed over, and documents are signed, sanctioned, and recorded. The chief features of this phase are as follows:

- Completion of all tasks according to the plan and scope.
- Ensuring execution of all processes of the project.
- Receiving the closing signal and approval from all concerned parties.

Because of its nature, this phase also offers the entire team a learning experience, helping them gain insight into project performance for future projects, typically referred to as lessons learned.

SIGNIFICANCE OF THE CLOSING PHASE

A formal closing phase ensures that vital details of the project have been annotated and addressed before submitting the deliverables. Timely last-minute corrections may prevent poor outcomes for the project team and a dissatisfied stakeholder. A proper closure prevents the following:

- Poor quality deliverables.
- Not having a follow on plan in place.

- Having liability issues like payment delays, incomplete or unaccepted deliverables, etc.
- Making errors on future projects.

A proper closure helps the project manager to transfer accurate deliverables to the client, which ensures that the final stakeholders have the knowledge, methods, and pertinent skills to use and manage the end product or service. This phase validates that the project is formally closed and no longer considered operational.

The project closure phase includes activities such as finalizing project documentation, conducting a post-project review, and transferring project deliverables to stakeholders. It ensures that the project meets official recommendations for closure and is the last crucial step in order to conclude a project.

CLOSING PHASE ACTIVITIES

The closing phase activities for the project manager include creating the closeout checklist to ensure nothing has been left unnoticed or unmanaged. It consists of the following:

Official Transference of Deliverables

The project manager must achieve completion and hand over deliverables to the client or stakeholders after checking the project plan to determine if the deliverables satisfy the plan.

Project Completion Confirmation

A project can be declared closed once all concerned parties agree, without which the project would continue indefinitely, possibly, receiving change requests by the client, in turn costing unnecessary time and resources. Approval signatures by all stakeholders regarding project completion and deliverables must be obtained, documented, and archived as proof of project closure.

Contracts and Document Reviews

After completing the project handover and receiving validation from the client/stakeholder, the project manager must close out any contracts and review the project documentation to check pending invoices and payments to all project participants and collaborators.

Release Resources

Resource release is a crucial task during the project closing phase. The team, being the most valuable internal resource, is released from obligations concerning the project. Additionally, any unused internal resources, such as budget, are released for reallocation. External resources contracted for the project have a period of performance specified in their contracts. To meet the terms and conditions of the contract, payments, and deliverables must be identified and fulfilled before closing the contract.

Review the Project

Reviewing the project is the most crucial aspect of project closure when successes, mistakes, and difficulties are assessed and analyzed for lessons learned in order to gain insight into future improvements.

Archiving Documents

Documents serve as valuable reference material for future projects and provide evidence of project processes and actions. As such, they should be treated with importance and care. Comprehensive and well-documented records may be necessary for legal purposes or at the request of stakeholders. Contracts, project plans, scope, costs, and schedules must be reviewed, completed, and indexed for archiving in the company's files for future reference. Accurate documentation of project performance and improvement opportunities can aid future similar projects.

Lessons Learned

Lessons learned involve documenting successes, failures, processes, and strategies used in a project. Proper documentation is crucial for capturing and recording these lessons, which can improve future project management practices. Comprehensive and well-documented records increase the likelihood of effectively capturing and utilizing lessons learned in future endeavors. This leads to more efficient and effective project management practices and better outcomes for organizations and stakeholders.

Lessons learned are useful for the future, particularly when new projects are beginning, and the team needs to dial back and look at what it has achieved in past projects, what has worked, and what hasn't. Also, a well-documented project file can be useful as a guide in filling in new project documents.

On the way to successful project completion, remember to review the performances of vital team members. For the project's benefit, note whether the performance meets overall project objectives. Also, take into account if the team had ample staff needed to finish requisite tasks.

Questions can be framed on project objectives, management support, organizational structure, and stakeholder involvement (Gersten, 2023).

Similarly, questions can be framed on planning, resources, cost, time, communications, and meetings. Some areas for reflection are as follows:

- Has the work accomplished on this project been properly documented?
- What was the discouraging aspect of the project?
- What was beneficial and advantageous for the project?
- What was successful, and what was not?
- What was not accomplished?
- As an afterthought, what things could have been done differently?

THE CHECKLIST

- Go through the project scope document, ensuring all listed requirements are completed.
- Ensure handing over the deliverables, signed and approved by the stakeholders.
- Obtain signatures for project documents by designated individuals, including pending contracts and agreements with contractors and vendors.
- Process the signed documents, release any final payments, and close any pending contracts.

- Collect all documents, including finalized project reports, and arrange and archive them for future reference.
- Use collected documents for lessons learned documentation, including feedback from stakeholders, to prevent making mistakes on similar issues in the future.
- Transition support individual assignment is necessary to steer the project following completion (Ray, 2022).
- Release or redistribute resources, including the team, equipment, space, etc.

PROJECT REVIEW

A project review meeting is held at the project's close, and all team members must be present. A representative from all its major areas must attend the meeting for larger projects.

A questionnaire session precedes the meeting to prepare the team members for the meeting's objectives. A proper review contains all aspects of project planning, execution, management decisions, finance, and organization concerning the project. The review will determine the successes and failures of the project lifecycle.

A project review meeting has well-defined objectives with standard questions based on the project's success and performance. The objectives are as follows:

- Learning from the experience and knowledge gained.
- Duplication of the successes in future projects
- Learning how to manage situations that did not go well
- Data collection and preservation for others' benefit.
- Pinpoint processes that require changes

END WITH A CELEBRATION

Vazquez, project manager for GNC Mexico, mentioned that celebrating project success ensured all team members understood their input was valued and connected with their customers' lives. He customarily congratulated all team members for their effort in the project and sometimes had food and beverages when the project delivery entailed hard work. A wrap-up project team selfie was an enjoyable must-have for the team (How Do You Celebrate Project Success? 2017).

A project closing party can serve as an official acknowledgment and celebration of the project's achievements and the professionals involved in its completion. The event's size and budget may vary, but it's common intentions include promoting team members, appreciating the project manager and personnel, and providing exposure. Such events can motivate team members to continue their best efforts in future projects with the organization.

An event can give visibility to the organization, which receives credence for its organizational strategy and efficient thinking from the stakeholders.

SUMMARY

- The closing phase helps the project manager transfer accurate deliverables to the client.
- This phase validates that the project is formally closed and no longer considered operational.
- The closing phase is used to review the entire project and for lessons learned.

7

EARNED VALUE MANAGEMENT & SWOT

E arned value management, or EVM, is a management system that provides quick visibility to issues concerning the project's cost and time when applied to all project management levels. For the project manager, using EVM facilitates vital decision-making. It eases work progress according to the baseline plan and informs about cost and time-related performance, besides giving data conducive to preventative management activities (What is Earned Value Management and Why is it Important? 2017).

Its benefits are:

- Providing more information than conventional project tracking methods.

- Gives an accurate prediction regarding the project's present stage and the remaining completion time
- The value-added approach gives better visibility and control to resolve problems earlier, allowing timely completion.
- Provides better communication of activities and accountability.

The tenet of EVM is that the value of a task is the same as the amount of budget funds allocated to complete the task.

- Planned value: the approved budget for a task to be finished by a fixed date.
- Earned value: the approved budget for the task completed in real-time by the set date.
- Actual costs: represents the actual costs for the work finished by the selected date.

The following indicators are used to describe the schedule and cost performance of the project using EVM:

- **Schedule variance (SV)**: measures of the difference between the work that was done and the amount of planned work. It shows if the project is on schedule.

- **Cost variance (CV)**: measures the difference between the budget amount for the work to be done and the actual amount spent for the performed work. It shows if the project is within the budget.
- **Schedule performance index (SPI)**: the ratio between the approved budget for the performed work and the planned budget. It gives a relative measure of time efficiency.
- **Cost performance index (CPI)**: the ratio between the approved budget for the performed work and the budget spent for the designated work. It is a relative measure of cost efficiency and is used to calculate the cost of the remaining task.

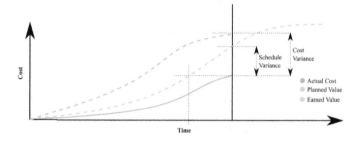

Image: Earned Value Management

SWOT ANALYSIS

A SWOT analysis is a planning tool designed by Albert Humphrey to identify the Strengths, Weaknesses, Opportunities, and Threats of a project. It provides a framework for the project's operational settings to correspond to the goals, objectives, and mission of the organization or business.

SWOT is frequently used for strategic or planning processes with an understanding of the situations of the project or organization, which helps with crucial decision-making. SWOT analysis states the project objective and identifies the internal and external factors that can support or oppose achieving that objective.

For management purposes, SWOT can help with self-evaluation quickly and more comprehensively. Its flexibility of application makes it a popular tool.

A proper SWOT analysis is a core knowledge component of project management; it is complex, requires time and resources, and requires a team effort for implementation. An inaccurate analysis leads to false assumptions, causing significant delays in efficient and timely decision-making regarding choosing other strategic options (SWOT Analysis, 2021).

The SWOT Components

The 'SWOT' captures data followed by the analysis. Its components are as follows:

- Strengths: positive internal attributes of the organization that are within its control
- Weaknesses: denote the areas where the organization can improve. They are internal factors within control, but they prevent the organization from reaching the desired goal.
- Opportunities: external factors that provide the reasons for the existence or development of the organization. They include the opportunities present in the environment that can mean success for the organization. Opportunities are identified by their time span.

- Threats: external factors that can jeopardize the organization's mission or function and are not within its control. The organization may develop contingency plans to cope with them if they occur. The risk factors can be categorized by their gravity and chances of occurrence.

Threats and opportunities are competitive forces that may appear in a competitive market scenario, while strengths and weaknesses are predictive factors and within control. Thus, they are value-added skills.

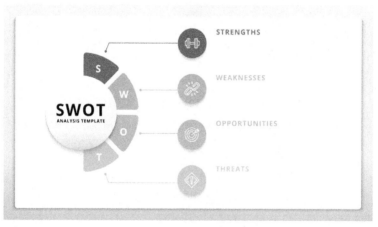

Image: SWOT Analysis Template

SUMMARY

Here is a rundown of the important points covered in this chapter:

- Earned value management provides quick visibility of the project's cost and time when applied to all project management levels.
- For the project manager, using EVM facilitates vital decision-making.
- A SWOT analysis is a planning tool designed by Albert Humphrey to identify the Strengths, Weaknesses, Opportunities, and Threats of a project.

With this, the end of the book is here. The next section will conclude the book and prepare project managers for their journey into a successful career field.

CONCLUSION

Projects start with an aim, a mission, or a problem that needs resolving. The project manager is at the helm of the project to conduct it efficiently within the stipulated budget and timeframe. The project manager defines the scope of the project, constructs the team, and makes the first few essential steps to initiate the project.

They have to follow through with all the phases of the project's lifecycle. The more things are thought of and planned in the beginning, the better the chances of surviving the storm that may come. Meticulous and systematic procedural steps ensure consideration of all areas of project management, given the likelihood that unforeseen circumstances can appear during the project's lifetime.

It is not without reason that most of the project's success depends on organized and heedful planning. Besides developing the project schedule, planning establishes the baseline of risk management procedures, roles, and responsibilities of individual stakeholders and sets the crucial milestones for the project. Communication is another vital area that is defined during the planning phase.

During the project execution phase, the project plan is put into action, and deliverables are produced. The project manager plays a crucial role in monitoring and controlling the project, ensuring that it stays on track with regard to the project schedule, budget, performance, and risk management parameters.

The project execution phase is the time for a project plan to be put into action and for deliverables to be generated. The project manager plays a vital role during this stage. They monitor and control the project, ensuring it stays on track in terms of the project schedule, budget, performance, and crucial risk management parameters.

Scope creep is a challenge that can derail a project and must be dealt with promptly. Project awareness can prevent the development of scope creep. At the same time, the project manager must motivate the team members and negotiate with the stakeholders on the different project issues.

The final phase is project closing, when the deliverables are handed over to the end users. This phase is hectic for the project manager, who must receive official approval for closure, prepare the final report, sign off the project formally, and close all project procedures and any outstanding documentation.

All documents must be archived into a data bank for reference. A postmortem on the project is always a good idea as it gives the team valuable lessons learned for future projects. Lessons learned, in turn, become great tools for future project teams to gain insight into all past project successes and failures.

Project management is undoubtedly challenging, but it is also exciting. Creative people take pride in their projects. New projects mean new challenges and different experiences. As a project manager, one should always be up for new ventures.

AUTHOR'S NOTE TO THE READERS

This book is designed to inspire project managers to reach their project management goals. By outlining proven methods and techniques that lead to favorable outcomes, readers will gain the knowledge and tools necessary to achieve successful project management. By combining the advice in this book with their own skills and abilities, readers will be well-positioned to achieve their goals. It's important to maintain clarity of goals and perseverance in order to ensure success. Remember, these two qualities are essential for any project manager's success, so embrace them and make them your allies. With the guidance of this book and your own determination, success in project management is within reach.

If reading this book brought valuable insight, please don't forget to leave a review on Amazon! Many thanks for following along, and I hope there was instrumental learning acquired along the way.

REFERENCES

REFERENCES

11 Reasons Why Projects Fail (And Solutions For Them). (2021, September 27). Blog SYDLE. https://www.sydle.com/blog/reasons-why-projects-fail--6151d64fde29ad2daaa6457e/

6 Project Constraints: Manage Them for Project Success [2023] • Asana. (2022, November 5). Asana. Retrieved March 22, 2023, from https://asana.com/resources/project-constraints

7 common causes of scope creep, and how to avoid them. (2023, January 12). Asana. Retrieved March 22, 2023, from https://asana.com/resources/what-is-scope-creep

Aldridge, E. A. (2022, June 27). How to Monitor Risk in Project Management. Project Management Academy Resources. Retrieved March 23, 2023, from https://projectmanagementacademy.net/resources/blog/how-to-monitor-risks/

APMG International. (2017, July 7). What is Earned Value Management and Why is it Important? https://apmg-international.com/article/what-earned-value-management-and-why-it-important

Aston, B. (2021, August 10). Why Is Project Management So Important To An Organization? The Digital Project Manager. https://thedigitalprojectmanager.com/personal/new-pm/why-is-project-management-important/

Aziz, E. E. (2015). Project closing: the small process group with big impact. Paper presented at PMI® Global Congress 2015—EMEA, London, England. Newtown Square, PA: Project Management Institute.

Becker, G. M. (2004). A practical risk management approach. Paper presented at PMI® Global Congress 2004—North America, Anaheim, CA. Newtown Square, PA: Project Management Institute.

Bierman. (2019, February 23). Evolving the function and expectations of the Project Manager. Evolving the Function and Expectations of the Project Manager. Retrieved March 22, 2023, from https://www. linkedin.com/pulse/evolving-function-expectations-project-manager-jennifer-bierman

Blackridge. (2022, February 7). What Is Project Logistics? A Simple Guide. Www.blackridgeresearch.com. https://www.blackridgere search.com/blog/what-is-project-logistics

Boogaard, K. (2022, May 24). What Is Hybrid Project Management? | Wrike. Www.wrike.com. https://www.wrike.com/blog/what-hybrid-project-management/

Brotherton, S. A., Fried, R. T., & Norman, E. S. (2008). Applying the work breakdown structure to the project management lifecycle. Paper presented at PMI® Global Congress 2008—North America, Denver, CO. Newtown Square, PA: Project Management Institute.

Caietti, N. (2019, May 30). 10 Strategies to Promote Successful Project Execution. ProjectManager.com. https://www.projectmanager. com/blog/project-execution

Celebrate Good Times: We Asked the Project Management Community: How Do You Celebrate Project Success? (2017). PM Network, 31(6), 20–21. https://www.pmi.org/learning/library/good-times-celebrate-project-success-10822.

Choma, A. A. & Bhat, S. (2010). Success vs. failure: what is the difference between the best and worst projects? Paper presented at PMI® Global Congress 2010—North America, Washington, DC. Newtown Square, PA: Project Management Institute.

Conduct A Project Review - Project Management Skills. (2023, March 22). Grist Project Management. Retrieved March 23, 2023, from https://www.gristprojectmanagement.us/skills/conduct-a-project-review.html

Coursera. (2021, September 1). 4 Phases of the Project Management Lifecycle Explained. Coursera. https://www.coursera.org/articles/project-management-lifecycle

CSPO, E. A., PMP, PMI-ACP, &. (2022, June 27). How to Monitor Risk in Project Management. Project Management Academy Resources. https://projectmanagementacademy.net/resources/blog/how-to-monitor-risks/

Dash, S. N. (2020, August 18). Work Breakdown Structure (WBS) in Traditional and Agile Life Cycles with MS Project. MPUG. https://www.mpug.com/work-breakdown-structure-wbs-in-traditional-and-agile-life-cycles-with-ms-project/

Eby, K. (2021, October 21). Project Controls: Processes and Plans | Smartsheet. Www.smartsheet.com. https://www.smartsheet.com/content/project-controls

Everitt, J. (2020, June 17). How to Conduct a SWOT Analysis in Project Management | Wrike. Www.wrike.com. https://www.wrike.com/blog/tips-swot-analysis-in-project-management/

Hardy-Valley, B. (2012, February 21). How to Run a Successful Project. Gallup.com. https://news.gallup.com/businessjournal/152756/run-successful-project.aspx

How Much Do Project Managers Make? (2022, December 21). Www.linkedin.com. https://www.linkedin.com/pulse/how-much-do-project-managers-make-get-hired-by-linkedin-news/

Jersak, M. (2023). This is Why a Risk Management Plan is Important. People First Project Management. https://peoplefirstprojectmanagement.com/this-is-why-a-risk-management-plan-is-important/

Keup, M. (2021, June 4). How to Create a Project Roadmap (Example Included). ProjectManager. https://www.projectmanager.com/blog/tips-for-project-roadmap

Kissflow. (2021a, January 24). What is Scope Creep? Causes and 5 Ways to Avoid it in Projects. Kissflow. https://kissflow.com/project/avoid-scope-creep-in-project/

Kissflow. (2021, February 25). Why Project Communication Management is Critical to Project Success. Kissflow. https://kissflow.com/project/communication-in-project-management/

Landau, P. (2023, March 1). Resource Management: Process, Tools & Techniques. ProjectManager. https://www.projectmanager.com/blog/quick-guide-resource-management

MacNeil, C. (2021, October 6). Project Initiation: the First Step to Successful Project Management • Asana. Asana. https://asana.com/resources/project-initiation

Malsam, W. (2023, February 16). Assembling a Project Team: Roles, Responsibilities & Best Practices. ProjectManager. https://www.projectmanager.com/blog/assemble-a-project-team

Martins, Julie. (2022, November 19). Create a Project Plan That Works for Your Team • Asana. Asana. https://asana.com/resources/project-management-plan

Miessler, D. (2019, April 21). The Difference Between Goals, Strategies, Metrics, OKRs, KPIs, and KRIs. Daniel Miessler. https://danielmiessler.com/blog/the-difference-between-goals-strategies-metrics-okrs-kpis-and-kris/

Monnappa, A. (2012, January 21). Project Scope Management and Its Importance in 2023 | simplilearn. Simplilearn.com. https://www.simplilearn.com/project-scope-management-importance-rar89-article

Montgomery, O. (2021, June 21). Rediscover the Strengths of Traditional Project Management. Www.capterra.com. https://www.capterra.com/resources/why-traditional-project-management-is-needed/

Narayan Dash, S. (2020, August 18). Work Breakdown Structure (WBS) in Traditional and Agile Life Cycles with MS Project | MPUG. MPUG. https://www.mpug.com/work-breakdown-structure-wbs-in-traditional-and-agile-life-cycles-with-ms-project/

Neumeyer, A. (n.d.). How to Plan a Project? — Follow these steps to launch your project. Tactical Project Manager. https://www.tacticalprojectmanager.com/how-to-start-a-project/

Neumeyer, A. (n.d.). Project phases - A practical overview (with real project examples). Tactical Project Manager. https://www.tacticalprojectmanager.com/the-project-phases-an-overview-with-real-examples/

O'Loughlin, E. (2018, June 19). Project Success Metrics: Keeping Projects on Time & on Budget. Www.capterra.com. https://www.capterra.com/resources/criteria-for-measuring-project-success/

Palmer. (2021, July 14). Communication techniques for effective project management. Communication Techniques for Effective Project Management. Retrieved March 23, 2023, from https://www.apm.org.uk/blog/communication-techniques-for-effective-project-management/

PMI. (2021). Pulse of the Profession Report. Retrieved March 23, 2023 from https://www.pmi.org/-/media/pmi/documents/public/pdf/learning/thought-leadership/pulse/pmi_pulse_2021.pdf

Project Management Demand: Career Opportunities. (2023, March 15). Project Management Demand: Career Opportunities. Retrieved March 31, 2023, from https://www.knowledgehut.com/blog/project-management/project-management-demand

Project Manager. (2022). Project Planning. ProjectManager. https://www.projectmanager.com/guides/project-planning

Project Roles & Responsibilities - UMass Boston. (2023). Project Roles & Responsibilities - UMass Boston. Retrieved March 22, 2023, from https://www.umb.edu/it/project_management_office/methodology/project_roles_responsibilities

Ray, S. (2022, February 15). 5 Steps to Project Closure (Checklist Included). ProjectManager. https://www.projectmanager.com/blog/project-closure

Runyon. (2022, February 18). Why "power skills" is the new term for soft skills in the hybrid work world - Thomson Reuters Institute. Thomson Reuters Institute. Retrieved March 22, 2023, from https://www.thomsonreuters.com/en-us/posts/legal/power-skills-rebranding/

Shaker, K. (2010). Why do projects really fail? PM Network, 24(7), 20–21.

Shenhar, A. (2000). Creating competitive advantage with Strategic Project Leadership™. Paper presented at Project Management Institute Annual Seminars & Symposium, Houston, TX. Newtown Square, PA: Project Management Institute. https://www.pmi.org/learning/library/competitive-advantage-strategic-project-leadership-554

SmartSuite. (2021, December 7). Goal vs Objective: 3 Key Differences

You Need to Know. Www.smartsuite.com. https://www.smartsuite.com/blog/goal-vs-objective

SWOT analysis: Factsheets. CIPD. (2022). Retrieved March 31, 2023, from https://www.cipd.co.uk/knowledge/strategy/organisational-development/swot-analysis-factsheet#gref

Teamwork. (2020, February 26). Project Management Methodologies – Everything You Need To Know. Www.teamwork.com. https://www.teamwork.com/project-management-guide/project-management-methodologies/

Thai. (2023, January 3). See the in's and out's of every project to better track your work. Asana. Retrieved March 23, 2023, from https://asana.com/resources/visual-project-management-kanban-timeline-calendar

Shaker, K. (2010). Why do projects really fail? PM Network, 24(7), 20–21. https://www.pmi.org/learning/library/identify-factors-cause-project-failure-2442

Sheffield, J. & Lemétayer, J. (2010). Critical success factors in project management methodology fit. Paper presented at PMI® Global Congress 2010—Asia Pacific, Melbourne, Victoria, Australia. Newtown Square, PA: Project Management Institute. https://www.pmi.org/learning/library/select-fitting-project-management-approach-6915

Smart Suite. (2021, December 7) Understanding the Difference Between Goals and Objectives in Project Planning and Management: A Guide to Setting SMART Goals and Objectives for Project Success. https://www.smartsuite.com/blog/goal-vs-objective. Retrieved March 22, 2023, from https://www.smartsuite.com/blog/goal-vs-objective

Usmani, F. (2022, June 13). 5 Whys for Root Cause Analysis: Definition, Example, and Template |. PM Study Circle. https://pmstudycircle.com/5-whys/

Usmani, F. (2022a, April 16). Project Objectives: Definition, Example & How to Write Project Objective |. PM Study Circle. https://pmstudycircle.com/project-objectives/

Westland, J. (2019, July 29). The 10 Project Management Knowledge

Areas. ProjectManager. https://www.projectmanager.com/blog/10-project-management-knowledge-areas

What Is a Project: Definition, Types, Key Features and More [Updated] | Simplilearn. (2020, September 29). Simplilearn.com. https://www.simplilearn.com/what-is-a-project-article

What Is Project Sequencing? (With Benefits and Tips). (2022, June 25). Indeed Career Guide. https://www.indeed.com/career-advice/career-development/project-sequencing

Williams, P. R. (2015). Visual project management. Paper presented at PMI® Global Congress 2015—EMEA, London, England. Newtown Square, PA: Project Management Institute.

Wootton, P. (2019). ProjectManagement.com - Key Performance Indicators. Projectmanagement.com. https://www.projectmanagement.com/wikis/345150/Key-Performance-Indicators

Printed in Great Britain
by Amazon

31107740R00136